W9-ADC-466

THE PHILOSOPHY

OF

F. W. J. SCHELLING

Studies in Phenomenology and Existential Philosophy

THE PHILOSOPHY

OF

F. W. J. SCHELLING

HISTORY, SYSTEM,
AND FREEDOM

Werner Marx

TRANSLATED BY

Thomas Nenon

INDIANA UNIVERSITY PRESS

BLOOMINGTON

Manufactured in the United States of America

Library of Congress Cataloging in Publication Data
Marx, Werner.
The philosophy of F.W.J. Schelling.
(Studies in phenomenology and existential philosophy)
Translation of: Schelling, Geschichte, System,
Freiheit.
Includes bibliographical references and indexes.
1. Schelling, Friedrich Wilhelm Joseph von, 1775–1854.
I. Title. II. Series.
B2898.M3813 1984   193   84-47706
ISBN 0-253-34445-X
1 2 3 4 5 88 87 86 85 84

In memory of
KARL LÖWITH

CONTENTS

FOREWORD

The figure of Schelling, prince of the romantics, has been too long over-
shadowed by that of Hegel, no doubt for more than one historical or
doctrinal reason. It is heartening, therefore, to perceive the growing interest in recapturing a realization and appreciation of the unique
thought of this most genial thinker, and to welcome with gratitude
Werner Marx's application of his very considerable interpretative skill
to this important task.

If the three fellow students at the Tübingen seminary—Hölderlin,
Hegel, and Schelling—swore eternal loyalty to the great ideal of the
French revolution, freedom, the remainder of their intellectual and spiritual life was indeed devoted to the development of their individually
different visions of its meaning. For the two philosophers the task became that of grasping the nature and reality of freedom within the context of necessity, a necessity laid down in the structure of life and history
previously interpreted by means of the teleo-logical ideas of classic
Greco-Roman thought and the Hebraic-Christian religious tradition,
that entire onto-theo-logical tradition with which in more recent times
Heidegger and those who have followed after him have found themselves at one and the same time pervaded and embattled. How is the
freedom of the human individual, for the sake of which the revolution
was fought and won, possible, if it is embedded in a process, natural on
the one hand and spiritually historical on the other, that runs with its
own immanent necessity? How can man's moral, aesthetic, and religious motives retain effective credibility when they are seen as phases
within stages of development in nature and history regulated by universal power or law?

This problem of his freedom confronted modern man at the beginning of the modern age and still remains most urgently pressing. The
poets and thinkers of the succeeding ages found their signal preoccupa-
tions precisely with this question. It is not without interest that Werner
Marx discovers his contemporary Habermas embroiled in the difficulties of the matter and finds it useful to project him and Schelling in

their mutual confrontations. But before Habermas the decisive movement into fundamental possibilities were made by Hegel and Schelling,
the former along the line of the concept, the latter along that of the intuition: *Begriff*, *Anschauung*, the two basic directions of movement of the
human understanding and, for the different idealisms, of the divine understanding itself in its process.

The concept, being logical, when essentially related to the telos as
end, necessarily turns around in its own circle of identity, departing
from and returning to itself in an eternal revolution. It was foreordained
that Hegel, partisan of the concept, should find his maturest thinking
take the form of an encyclopedia, the all-inclusive circular system whose
prime significance lies precisely in circling around forever within itself,
the system *as* system. Equally foreordained was it that logic, the essential form of conceptual thinking, should be the dominant mode in
which the system's structure, mechanism, and process should be cast—
and that God should be envisioned as the supreme logician.

At the beginning, in the middle, and in the end Hegel was the sys-
tematist, for whose thought everything found its due place—freedom
too—within the concept's circular rhythm. But the freedom constituted
in this system was God's, not man's: God's being by and with himself,
his *Beisichselbstsein*, which man can reproduce only with imperfections
and always only within God's own self-presence. The problem of the
reality of the human individual's finite freedom remains and it is to this
problem that Schelling found himself compelled to orient his thought.
How can human freedom subsist in relation to the eternal freedom?

If Hegel was the supreme conceptualist, Schelling was the supreme
intuitionist. In his latest years Schelling characterized Hegel's thought
as the purely rational and therefore purely negative philosophy, to
which he opposed his own as the positive philosophy. If Hegel stayed
with the concept in its ringed self-return, Schelling (who even ventured
to call himself an empiricist) broke through the ring to recover in intuition the real presence of the existent. God (the Gods) could not be a
conceptual circle for him but a living presence, God of the living. In his
youth the dominant mode of realization of this presence and the dominant mode of imagining the reality of freedom was that of art, the aesthetic dimension. During the period of transcendental idealism he
understood art as the organon of philosophical thought, guided by the
philosopher's intuition rather than by conceptual abstractions. In the

middle years Schelling moved from the dominion of art to the dominion of religion while yet retaining the two in the singular union granted by mythology. The first part of positive philosophy had to be the philosophy of mythology. And Schelling looked forward to, yearned for, a new realization of religion by means of a new mythical intuition of truth to recapture the life that had worn itself out in its Christian form.

The path of Schelling's thought is sometimes described as following through a sequence of stages, from an early Fichtean transcendental idealism and its associated philosophy of nature, through the doctrine of absolute identity, to the philosophy of freedom and then the positive philosophy of religion in its mythological and theosophical character. If there is a real break, it comes most plausibly with the passage from the period of identity to that of freedom. In the period of transcendental idealism and philosophy of nature and in the succeeding period of identity, human life and its processes remained a harmonious part of the playing out of the divinely determined history of revelation and salvation. The aesthetic dimension was eminently suited to this vision, already embodied in the system of transcendental idealism in the image of God as author of a drama in which humans participate not only as actors but also as co-authors. Such an idyllic, optimistic picture was agreeable to a relatively innocent youth but hardly to the man who encountered in life, with growing acuteness, the reality of evil, especially as it is brought about by humans themselves, his own self not excluded. Not man as cooperant with God but man as rebel against God, the finite center that sets itself up against the absolute divine center of love—this is the image that takes shape as Schelling experiences the inescapable education of thought by its intuitional confrontation with itself and its world.

In his writings this transition is perhaps most easily seen in the movement from *Philosophy and Religion* (1804) to the masterpiece, *Philosophical Inquiries into the Essence of Human Freedom* (1809). With the essay on freedom Schelling turns definitively toward the dark reality of man's difference from God, the difference of existence centered upon the finitude of the human self in its opposition to the centered infinitude of love. The human difference is no part of a mere play of the divinity with its own forms or creations but a real difference grounded in something real within the divinity that nevertheless rebels against its subordination there.

This move is at the same time a move out of the circling system of human reason, which brought to culmination the onto-theo-logical tradition of the West, back into the existential reality of the finite human spirit embroiled in evil's self-victimization and the struggle against it. Hegel early thought he had encompassed Schelling's thinking as having the form of speculative reflection, that is to say, the form of the identity of identity and difference. Did Hegel ever come to realize the real possibility of thought that finds itself marked as the difference of identity and difference? With Schelling's essay on human freedom, that overarching difference, no longer mere speculation nor mere reflection but a fiery existence grounded in the nature of the divine existence, flares into intuitionable presence. With this burning presence the face of evil shows itself plainly to the being who is finitely free and there is initiated a stage of thought, still not completed in our time, in which the inescapable ambiguities of freedom and necessity, evil and the problematic nature of its overcoming, haunt us unceasingly and ever more trenchantly.

ALBERT HOFSTADTER

TRANSLATOR'S NOTE

The method of quotation employed in the original German edition has been retained and may require some explanation. In order to reduce the number of footnotes, the majority of references to primary texts have been incorporated into the text, whereby the volume and page number of a quoted author's works are given in a footnote immediately following the quotation. A roman numeral refers to the volume, an arabic numeral to the page. Wherever a page number appears alone, the quotation is taken from the last mentioned volume or work. Quotations from Schelling, Hegel, and Habermas were compared with the available English translations, but for the sake of uniformity the translations of these quotations are my own. Important German terms have often been included in parentheses so that the reader can judge the appropriateness of the given translation.

Quotations were taken from the following editions:

F. W. J. Schelling, *Werke*, ed. M. Schröter (Munich, 1927). (The page and volume numbers listed, however, refer to the original edition by K. F. A. Schelling. The page numbers of the original are also given in the margins of the various English translations of Schelling's works.)

G. W. F. Hegel, *Werke*, ed. Verein von Freunde des Verewigten (Berlin, 1932).

G. W. F. Hegel, *Phänomenologie des Geistes*, ed. J. Hoffmeister (Hamburg, 1952). (The page number of the English translation by A. V. Miller, *The Phenomenology of Spirit* [Oxford, 1977], is listed in italics.)

Jürgen Habermas, *Erkenntnis und Interesse* (Frankfurt, 1973). (The page number of the English translation by J. Shapiro, *Knowledge and Human Interest* [Boston, 1971], is listed in italics.)

All other works cited are listed in the notes.

I would like to express my gratitude here to Dennis Schmidt, David Krell, and John Sallis for their invaluable assistance during the course of this translation. Most especially, I am indebted to Reginald Lilly for his numerous helpful suggestions and to the author for his constructive criticism and encouragement at all times in the preparation of this English edition.

THOMAS NENON

INTRODUCTION

The task and method of philosophy have become questionable in our age and, along with them, philosophy's traditional principles, categories, and standards. They no longer seem compatible with our own self-understanding or with our knowledge of earth, of life, and of the "laws" of nature. The predominant conviction is that metaphysical categories and the construction of metaphysical systems are things of the past. But at present there is no new fundamental view and therefore no conception of the task and method of philosophy which would be able to provide standards for the philosophical enterprise. We have not found any new categories.

At the sme time, old questions present themselves ever anew, and in spite of tendencies to discount the importance of history for modern science, the nature and meaning of history still present problems for our "historical consciousness." The danger in our present situation is that traditional categories are often employed in the attempt to solve this kind of problem, but that the intellectual presuppositions that provide the basis for these categories are renounced, either explicitly or implicitly.

The first section of this book attempts to illustrate this danger by means of an example. It explores the unique way in which Schelling conceived of history as determined by the relationship between freedom and necessity. In light of this conception, a contemporary theory of history is then examined in order to demonstrate that it operates with precisely those traditional categories whose presuppositions it has abandoned.

Even today, the complete rejection of the metaphysical tradition is still influenced by various anti-idealistic movements that arose during the last century and continued into the first half of this century. What was common to all of these movements was their opposition to Hegel's conviction that a system must be developed "from the concept" [aus dem Begriff]. It has been all but forgotten that, at approximately the same time that Hegel presented the Phenomenology of Spirit as the first part of such a system, Schelling elaborated a system based on a completely different principle, namely "self-intuition" [*Selbstanschauung*]. Especially in an age that is finding its way back to the notion of a system—even if for the most part in the form of theories of science or within a functionalistic sociological framework—it is important that we be reminded of this conceptual possibility. The second section thus contrasts Schelling's *System of Transcendental Idealism* with Hegel's *Phenomenology of Spirit* in order to re-emphasize the role that intuition and self-intuition can play in the construction of a system.

The present movement aimed at a renaissance of practical philosophy indicates that we are still disturbed by the question concerning the nature of freedom. It shows that the question concerning the "good," whether as a principle of conduct or the problem of the "good life," remains unsolved. Nor has a satisfactory response to the·question concerning the meaning and role of "evil" been found. The third section therefore interprets Schelling's *Philosophical Inquiries into the Essence of Human Freedom*, which provided answers to these questions from a standpoint within the metaphysical tradition and christological mysticism. These answers may serve as an admonition for endeavors in contemporary ethics: whatever modern terms may be used, the definitions of good and evil lack foundation if they are not viewed in reference to an absolute.

THE PHILOSOPHY

OF

F. W. J. SCHELLING

1

The Fundamental Notions
in Schelling's and Habermas's
Conceptions of History

I

THIS SECTION is intended as a portrayal and an analysis of the "concept of history," which the young Schelling developed in his *System of Transcendental Idealism* (1800). In his development of this concept, Schelling was the first to introduce history as the pivotal issue in German Idealism.

Such an effort to reconsider a traditional philosophy of history is immediately confronted with the objection that it cannot help but be irrelevant to a philosophical interpretation of history that could be convincing in the modern age, and it seems impossible that it could be considered relevant to current historiography. It would indeed be a mistake if one failed to recognize that the traditional foundation on which Schelling's entire enterprise is based can no longer correspond to our modern historical consciousness or to our conception of man and the world, for they have been too greatly transformed in our technological age. But which foundation is it then that sets the standards for current philosophical and scientific thought and for our ordinary conduct? Do we have any conception at all of such a foundation? It is the particular fate of our generation to live between tradition and another beginning with a new foundation.[1] We live in an age in which the previous categories of knowledge and the traditional standards of ethical conduct have been called into question or have even begun to disappear, although no new ones have arisen to take their place. We can bear our fate in full consciousness only if we recognize that the task of philosophy today consists in keeping the traditional foundations in view from the vantage point of the present when considering any new philosophical conceptions. We must examine whether and to what extent these new conceptions, if they are consistent in themselves, are only operatively applying traditional categories or whether they exhibit something that might lead to a new foundation.

Accordingly, I have selected the earlier Schelling's concept of history as opposed to his later ones simply because it lends itself more easily to the exposition of various traditional basic ideas on the matter. I have also chosen it as opposed to Hegel's concept, even though the latter was more significant in terms of historical influence, because an examination of Schelling's concept can show how the influence of certain modern tendencies led to a fundamental difficulty within the traditional framework. And this difficulty can be taken as an indication of certain inadequacies within the traditional framework. I shall then examine a contemporary concept of history in light of the fundamental categories and basic ideas that we are able to discover in Schelling's concept of history. The contemporary concept of history to be analysed is that developed by Jürgen Habermas, because it is in our opinion characteristic of the current discussion regarding history.

It may seem surprising that it was Schelling, a student of Fichte, who was the first in German Idealism to make history a theme of transcendental philosophy. Fichte, however, had spoken of history only in a sense that has nothing to do with the usual one, in the sense of a logical genesis that proceeds from the principle of self-consciousness and unfolds all the possibilities for thought contained in the principle, as demonstrated in his *Science of Knowledge* (1794). Subsequently in the *System of Transcendental Idealism* (1800), the younger Schelling also made use of such a genesis in order to develop the theoretical and practical faculties of the subject, more specifically, in order to trace the manner in which they take shape for the subject outside of itself, the manner in which they become "objective." In so doing, he reached the point where he was confronted with the task of showing how the subject's will becomes objective. One such objectivation then turned out to be history. This fact, and probably also a strong historical, even eschatological consciousness that he shared with his closest friends, prompted Schelling to inquire into the "concept of history" and to determine its various moments.

Which concept of history did Schelling initially develop? History "is only there," he wrote, "where One Ideal among endlessly many deviations is so realized that, though the particular individual does not congrue with it, the whole certainly does" (III, 588). Such a "realization" of the One Ideal is possible only for man. For man is a creature whose being, like that of animals, has the character of a species [*Gattüngswesen*], but in contrast to animals, man is capable of remaining conscious of One Ideal, One Purpose in history. The element of continuity necessary for any concept of history was supposed to be guaranteed by man's capability for tradition: individuals are able to hand down the Ideal to one another. More precisely, each succeeding individual was supposed to be able to commence where the previous individual left off. And therefore, for Schelling, the course of history proceeded not only continuously, but also progressively. The species mankind gradually approached the Ideal, although one could prove that the Ideal finally would be attained neither by means of experience nor by means of a theoretical a priori. For Schelling, this was an "eternal article of faith for the active and effective human being" (593), (cf. below p. 59).

What was this "One Ideal?" Or, we might ask with Schelling, what is the "only true object of history" (592)? His answer was that it is the gradual formation of a cosmopolitan legal constitution, of a legal order that would be valid not only for small groups or for a particular state. This legal order would rather unite the sovereign states, each of which would be organized according to the principle of the division of powers, into an international federation of cultured nations. And these cultured nations would have all subjected themselves to laws that guaranteed the existence of all states. Such a universal cosmopolitan constitution was considered "the only basis for history" (ibid.). It is well known that this ideal, dominant in the age of Enlightenment, had already been proposed by others before Schelling, in particular by Kant. Schelling's system, however, presented itself as the genesis of the principle of self-consciousness in its process of objectivation. Why, then, did Schelling view the cosmopolitan constitution as the One Ideal that must be realized?

The preceding deductions in part 4 of Schelling's *System of Transcendental Idealism*, the system of practical philosophy, demonstrated that the faculty of self-determination or freedom constitutes the essence of self-consciousness. If this is its essence, Schelling concluded, then no individual could continue to exist without a guarantee of freedom.

Therefore, in order to maintain this "holiest of all things," individual freedom, the species was constrained to organize itself, to construct an order that was governed by laws. It was necessary to introduce the "constraint of an inviolable law, so that collective interaction cannot possibly abolish the individual's freedom" (582). Schelling called this organization according to legal constitution a "second and higher" nature. He called it a "nature" because, at least externally, it was thought of as determined by the same category that rules visible nature: the category of necessity, a point that will be very important in the subsequent investigations. Just as Descartes had been the first to consider nature as an order that fulfills itself according to blind and unconscious mechanical laws not dependent on some mind, so for Schelling, a legal order had to function "like a machine." From the very outset, it had to be constructed for certain cases and then function blindly as soon as these cases arose. Nevertheless, the legal order was of course considered "superior" to visible nature because it had been constituted by the species "on the behalf of freedom."

Schelling asked whether we can at least "believe" (cf. p. 592) that this One Ideal of a cosmopolitan constitution will ever be realized. Can we believe that universal history leads to the complete assurance of individual freedom? His answer was that we can believe this only if we think that "a blind necessity dominates which objectively confers to freedom that which never would have been possible through freedom alone" (597). The blind necessity to which Schelling refers here is the necessity of a lawfulness, a necessity that determines the course of history and proceeds completely independently of individuals and states—over their heads, so to speak. Schelling thus saw two aspects in the concept of history that were independent of one another: on the one hand, the play of freedom, and on the other, the necessity in history's occurrence that binds its beginning and its end. Schelling, however, was not content with a mere description of this state of affairs. Rather, he referred it back to its conceptual elements in order to show them in their contradiction, and he then searched until a possibility for the resolution of this contradiction could be found. Before we further discuss how Schelling developed this problem within a transcendental philosophical framework, however, the basic ideas involved in the issues discussed up to this point should be presented, and an attempt should be made to determine their "meaning." For, from this vantage point the domain and the limits of the traditional foundation show themselves quite clearly.

Telos was one of the basic ideas involved here. This notion served as the background against which Schelling had conceived of the previously mentioned contradiction in the concept of history. *Telos* was taken here in the sense that it had gained in the history of Western thought by being translated as "*causa finalis*," and later, under the influence of eschatological ideas, into the German "Ziel" (goal), "Zweck" (purpose), and "Sinn" (meaning).[2] An end—understood as "a goal that has been reached," "a purpose that has been fulfilled," or as "the meaning"—determines the beginning and all stages in the development of a process that leads up to the end. An end, when taken as a cause, implies that something is predisposed in the initial and in each subsequent stage and presupposed as a real possibility. This form then proceeds to present itself, to become increasingly effective, and thus to become actually existent. In this manner, the end acts as the highest point that draws the beginning and all lower stages up into itself as stages of development. At the same time, it returns back into the beginning, from whence the presupposed conditions of the development strove, by "acting purposefully" toward completion, that is toward its purposeful, completely realized goal. *Telos* thus has the structure of a continual movement that realizes and completes itself in the form of a circle.

Schelling's notion of history was conceived of in accordance with the Greek conception of *telos* insofar as its "realization" is indeed a movement that proceeds from a beginning toward a goal and purpose. This goal was thought of as that highest point that determines and directs each stage of development from the very beginning, and compels each of these initial presuppositions to complete and fulfill itself purposefully in this goal. Later, of course, we shall have to deal with the influences in the history of thought that led *telos* to be transformed into an *eschaton*, since the notion of "progress," which characterized Schelling's concept of history, was not thought of as a movement proceeding circularly within itself, but rather in terms of an irreversible, nonrepeatable movement toward a point that lies in the future, an *eschaton*.

We should recall, first of all, that Aristotle introduced the concept of *telos* in his attempt to determine the essence of *physis*, of nature.[3] From the outset, however, nature was not for him matter without any soul, as it had been for Democritus. It was rather the living *entelechia* of an organism through which this organism develops its predisposed possibility, *dynamis*, to its determinant limits and thus renders this possibility manifest in its completion. The compelling force active in the movement of *telos* was viewed as having the character of an event, in that it asserts itself independently of, and often in opposition to, the conscious freedom of human beings in guiding this movement toward its *telos*, its goal. This characteristic was one of the elements that entered into the meaning of the determination "necessity."

It is important here to remain conscious of the fact that in Greek thought the determination of *telos* emerged in unity with two other key thoughts in our tradition, namely *nous* and *logos*. The pre-Socratics understood them as the illuminating and ordering powers. Plato and Aristotle conceived of them through the notion of the "idea" or "form," *eidos*. For them, *nous* and *logos* were the foundation for the predominance of the ideal over the material in the universe. Because *nous* and *logos* can be thought of as self-developing, insofar as the meaning of a whole gradually brings itself forth and fulfills itself through its parts, they have always been conceived of together with the determination of *telos*. One must, however, be mindful of the fact that the character of the constraint which resides in mental, logical acts, is of a different sort from that which is based on a development determined solely by *telos*. The stringency of *logos*, of thought, lies in its property of organizing an event so that hierarchy, divisions, and combinations result, and in the fact that it does this with complete transparency. This characteristic feature was also included in the meaning of "necessity."

It is well established that in the development of Western thought, it is the modern age that first witnessed the emergence of *logos* as the principle of self-consciousness, of subjectivity. *Logos* is no longer seen as reigning over the whole of the universe, nor is it, as it had been for the Scholastics, the divine law. It is now seen as "residing" in the "I," the conscious subject that attains indubitable certainty with regard to its own being, and thus with regard to its conceptual knowing. This rational subject is able to determine itself as effecting general laws through *logos*. *Logos* comes to denote a principle that makes possible and provides the foundation for all experiences. It becomes the founding principle of subjectivity that shows itself on the one hand in concepts, and on the other hand in freedom: not merely in freedom from the constraints of nature, but rather in the freedom of self-determination, autonomy. If this is taken to be the case, then what happens to the character of the constraining force, which we have said is proper to *logos*; a force that we determined to be the stringency of a directing and ordering necessity; a force that, when conceived of together with *telos*, takes on the character of an "irresistible urge" [*Drang*]? How can both freedom and necessity be contained in *logos*, not to mention in *teleo-logos*? Is this not a contradiction? It is indeed, and this is precisely the contradiction with which Schelling was confronted when he attempted to develop a concept of history based on "teleo-logical" subjectivity.

II

How DID Schelling conceive of the resolution of this contradiction? He himself termed the solution to this question the "supreme" problem of transcendental philosophy (594). We must remember that for Schelling the determinations within a transcendental framework were always just the foundation for more general convictions that are presupposed and adopted apart from philosophy. He presented the relationship between freedom and necessity as an example. Generally and unphilosophically, people speak of a "hidden necessity" that is given different names, "sometimes fate, sometimes providence" (ibid.). People think they feel the intervention of fate in their actions, in the success or failure of their enterprises. They think they notice a special relationship between fate and their freedom, especially when they become aware that their presumably free actions effect something that they did not want at all, or when they experience the failure of precisely that which they had planned, intended, and willed with all their might.

In any case, the general understanding of things is that the intentions that various individuals have in their actions tend toward something that cannot be realized by them alone, but only by the whole species. This would mean that the success of an individual's actions is dependent on the wills of all other individuals. Is it not necessary to disregard all individual plans and actions completely, as well as the effects of these actions, if we want to become conscious of the enigma that in history something comes to be that results without regard or even in opposition to the wills of those who act? According to the general understanding of things it indeed appears as if there were something that, without the assistance of individuals, slowly and steadily emerges out of a "hidden necessity" according to a "natural law," something that could never have been realized through the willing of individuals. In spite of this experience of a hidden necessity, the individual who is about to act retains a steadfast conviction of the freedom of his actions since this conviction is in fact the condition for the possibility of the action itself. As Schelling ascertained in the introduction to his *System of Transcendental Idealism*, in reference to the two "absolute prejudices" (344), both of these convictions, the conviction in the necessary determination of the ideal as well as the conviction in the free ability to realize it, are "deeply embedded in human understanding" (346). From this contradiction it follows that the historically active individual's consciousness, which is the object of transcendental reflection, is determined at one and the same time by the consciousness of necessity and the consciousness of freedom.

Transcendental philosophy is thus presented with the task of explaining the coexistence of such a development according to "natural law" (necessity) with the unrestricted expression of freedom. It has to answer the question of how something absolutely objective and common to all intelligent beings, something that arises without the assistance of anything subjective, can be conceived of together with the realization of freedom. A transcendental philosophy that proceeds from the principle of a self-determining self-consciousness, and that sets itself the task of presenting the genesis of this self-consciousness such that all of the "possibilities for thought" [*Denkmöglichkeiten*] lying within it can be unfolded, must explain how there can be something objective for this self-consciousness, something that is not constituted by freely determining, conscious actions.

It is precisely Schelling's philosophy, however, that is able to conceive how something "without consciousness" [*Bewusstloses*] constitutes itself for the philosopher's consciousness. The constitution of visible nature, especially of matter, shows itself to the philosopher as being "without consciousness." The philosopher then raises these products of unconscious "intuition" to the level of concept. He thus demonstrates how the unconscious execution of the species' intuition constitutes the objective side of history. The transcendental philosopher, who is able to reconstruct the genesis of objectivity, recognizes that all supposedly free actions that by nature are contradictory, are synthesized into something objective. This "objectivity" is that which appears to all individuals as "common to everyone," that which guides "all human actions to One harmonic Goal." Schelling determined this unconscious, self-fulfilling production as an "absolute synthesis." It denotes the lawfulness, the necessity that unphilosophical, general consciousness has traditionally understood as a hidden necessity—as fate, as the plan of nature, or the plan of "providence." Philosophers conceive of it in the notion of "predetermination." The transcendental philosopher, however, cannot remain content with having conceptualized this lawfulness as an absolute "synthesis," for the fact still must be explained "how the harmony is established between the objective element, which in complete independence from freedom brings forth its products, and the *freely determining element*" (599). Above all, there is no explanation for the fact that a lasting correspondence obtains between that which is absolutely free and that which, realizing itself wholly independently of freedom, is lawful. How can this be explained?

This is the point where Schelling began to think "speculatively." He realized that a kind of thinking must be employed here that does not orient itself toward that which is already given, but that rather takes its direction from the consistency that rules in the domain of thought. This thought experiences the necessity to develop the meaningful contents lying in the determinations of thought, and to take these alone as its guide. Hegel later developed the dialectical method in this manner, especially in his presentation of it in the *Science of Logic*. He demonstrated once and for all that, quite independently of any sort of given objects, thought can disclose the contents of meaning that "in themselves" [*an sich*] lie in the determinations of thought (the *thesis*). Furthermore, the meanings thus disclosed present a contradiction (*antithesis*) to the undisclosed meanings. If thinking pursues this contradiction to the utmost, this leads to a reconciliation, a *synthesis*.

Schelling's transcendental philosophical thought did not explicitly understand itself as being dialectical in a methodological sense. But within the realm of thought, it did already seek to reconcile the one side, absolute freedom, with the other side, absolute lawfulness. Leibniz had speculatively employed the same idea in reference to Geulincx's example of different clocks running parallel to one another as the "pre-established harmony" of independently existing substances or monads. Schelling reconciled both sides and explained them to be "identical" in this sense of a pre-established harmony, and thereby sought to preserve

their independence. "Identity" was one of the determinations introduced here that belongs to the dimension of speculative thought. With
the aid of this determination Schelling attempted to grasp that which
lies beyond finite appearances. And it was exactly at this point and with
the help of this determination that the transition was made from the
sphere of finitude, within which the concept of history interacts with
the elements of necessity and freedom, to the infinite sphere that lies
beyond consciousness. Schelling recognized that freedom and necessity
(lawfulness) would remain in an unbearable contradiction in spite of
their identity as a pre-established harmony if they were not derived
from an "absolute identity," and if they had not been grounded in such
an identity as their first principle or "ground" [*Grund*].

He tried to illustrate this ground by means of the metaphors "source"
[*Quelle*] and invisible "root" [*Wurzel*] (600). "Absolute identity" was
posited as the "condition for all consciousness" and for the inherent duplicity between knowing and the known. Absolute identity itself lay beyond all duplicity as its condition. A year later Schelling termed this
absolute identity "indifference,"[4] on account of its independence from
the sphere of finitude. Whereas Hegel conceived of an identity that is
not beyond finitude, but that rather mediated itself into the sphere of
finitude, into the sphere of the nonidentity of knowledge, in order to
become a synthetic unity by emerging out of this sphere and by being
fulfilled by it (see below pp. 35, 44–45).

Schelling thought the "ground" of lawfulness was freedom, and that
the freedom of objectivity's lawfulness was the ground of the harmony
between the two sides. For religious thought, however, this had been
nothing other than God. Thus, it was the plan of providence that philosophy conceived of in history's lawfulness. Divine providence was
said to show itself in traces "which, like the weavings of an unknown
hand, permeate the free play of willful choice [*Willkür*] in history"
(III, 601).

We have seen that the constraint of necessity has a twofold character
that lies in the modern comprehension of *logos*, of subjectivity in its traditional connection with *telos*. At the same time, it also contains the opposite of this constraint in total autonomy, freedom. Recently, philosophy is repeatedly confronted with the task of reconciling this opposition
if the subject is not to perish in the face of its own contradiction. As
long as contemporary philosophy still thinks "theologically," it seems

that it can indeed resolve this contradiction. This can be accomplished by demonstrating how these determinations manifest themselves in history when set in reference to God. *Logos* is then traced back into *theos*. This is the Aristotelian tradition: where the "ontological" question was posed for the first time, the *logos* of beings as beings already had a "theological character."[5]

Here I would like to interrupt these investigations briefly in order to show that the epoch in which Schelling philosophized was also decisively determined by "theo-logical" presuppositions, and that the fundamental determinations that he operatively employed have a theological character.

III

WE HAVE determined *logos* and *telos*, the foundations of Greek thought, to be the basic notions that, together with the modern fundamental idea of subjectivity, formed the basis for Schelling's "Philosophy of History." At this point, however, it should be emphasized that the Greeks themselves never wrote philosophies of history. They inquired into the *logos* of the *cosmos*. They recognized, of course, that all bodies in the sublunar realm are perishable. The fact that everything worldly—people, animals, things—"come to be and perish" [*genesis et pthora*]—was a fundamental experience for them, and this explains their inquiry into the essence of movement, matter, and time. Their thought was, however, also motivated by a second, much stronger fundamental experience, namely that in spite of all perishableness, chaos does not dominate, but rather all being is ordered (*taxis*). There is a beautiful structuredness, and this is the cosmos, the world. This experience probably arose due to the sight of the *uranos*, the starry firmament that overarches the islands of Greece. It presents itself to the eye as immutably bound (*peras*), as something without beginning and imperishable (*aidiai, aei*), and as a true illustration of order. More importantly, this perceptible order is not something inflexible and immobile, but is rather a manifestly dynamic order. The great heavenly bodies—the sun, the moon, the stars—in their rhythmic revolutions are the source of the yearly cycles on earth and manifest the recurrence of the seasons and the alternation from day to night.

Through this perceptible paradigm of the unity of order and movement, the Greeks conceived of the ideal of being as a synthesis of being and becoming, and they thought of this synthesis as an eternal recurrence of sameness in which everything that emerges reverts back to its beginnings. This cosmic view of the world did not allow the thought of a "philosophy of history." As Karl Löwith in particular has shown, the occasion for the beginning of a philosophy of history can be found in the development of monotheism into messianism as found in Jewish prophecy and in the Christian idea of a final goal in the history of redemption.[6] The passionate expectation of a kingdom in which the divine moral law would be reality and the Christian hope of a final judgment and a second coming of Christ were directed toward a future and final goal and borne by an unconditioned faith. These were the ideas that served as the foundations of a "philosophy of history" that inquired into the meaning of history, a meaning that for the church fathers was guaranteed by the revealed plan of providence. In its recent development, the philosophy of history was supported by the optimistic world view of the Renaissance and post-Renaissance. Vico's *Scienzia Nuova* initiated a transformation in the speculative theological presuppositions that continued throughout the Enlightenment with its faith in progress. The time became ripe for *Ideas Concerning the Philosophy of a History of Mankind* [*Ideen zur Philosophie der Geschichte der Menschheit*]. Under this title in 1774 Herder—in accordance with Lessing's earlier observations—posited his basic tenet that it is not only the world of nature that fulfills itself truly and necessarily in conformity to eternal laws, but that history also fulfills itself in this manner and leads humanity to a predetermined perfection. The Greek, or Platonic-Aristotelian, tradition of thought that we have sketched, was invoked here. It must be stressed in this case, however, that it was on the basis of the Scholastic tradition's understanding of *nous* and *logos* that the Christian God was conceived as mind. It was this God, thought of as mind, who, in creating the world, released from himself those ideas that previously had found their essence in him, and in so doing they became the real powers out of which being emerged. Being was revelation, the revelation of God; the world was *explicatio Dei*. The most important aspect of this process of the idea's self-realization was now seen in history, but history was conceived as operating in accordance with the basic theological ideas adopted from Greek thought, because their determination involved a kind of necessity suited to the Christian religious view. All of this was then taken up into the transcendental conception of a logic of the subject. Providence's plan was to be deduced from the transcendental logic of the subject, a logic that demanded the absence of contradiction in spite of the empirical, contradictory course of history. The opinion that Hegel expressed on this matter in all of his lectures on the philosophy of history is well known. He rejected as a contemptible oriental idea the view that history is a "slaughterhouse" where "the happiness of nations, the wisdom of states, and the virtue of individuals have been sacrificed."[7] He pointed instead to the Western idea that one should not merely be resigned to one's fate, but rather that history is a history of spirit or mind, *Geist*. This mental or rational conception of history had to assume the task of Christian religion in portraying history's progressive, self-completing process toward a final purpose as a "theodicy" (IX, 24ff.). In order to be able to consistently present such a conception of necessity dominant in the rational plan of the "world spirit," *Weltgeist*, Hegel even resorted to the idea of the "cunning of reason" [*List der Vernuft*] (83, *33*).

The character of the necessity dominant here can be adequately understood only if one is mindful of the fact that for Hegel the whole event of history was concerned with the pathway of divine self-revelation working in divine ideas. The constraint inherent in *logos* was thus endowed with a particular fundamental trait in addition to those we have already discussed. This trait had its origin in the sphere of the "holy," a sphere that lies beyond any constraint that can be humanly understood. It is obvious that such a conception of necessity also led to a transformation in the concept of "freedom." Freedom no longer referred to decision, choice, or the proposal of something individual or even new, but to the voluntary acceptance of necessity. A freedom that acknowledges the lawfulness inherent in the development of *logos*, which devotes itself to "the issue" [*der Sache*], is in reality no longer a freedom opposed to necessity. It is interesting for our problem here to note that Hegel never really solved the problem of the contradiction between necessity and freedom. One might say that instead he "eliminated" it. By contrast, Schelling, in his major work, *Philosophical Inquiries into the Essence of Human Freedom* (1809), truly posed the question concerning the contradiction between freedom and necessity. In this treatise it becomes clear that Schelling viewed the essence of freedom as residing in finite human freedom that must choose between good and evil (cf. pp. 78–79). Since this present study is devoted to Schelling's concept of *history*, however, we must now return to our original topic.

IV

IT CAN be said that from beginning to end, Schelling's philosophical thought revolved around the problem of the relationship between freedom and necessity. It is certain that this question became more pressing for him after he composed those pages in the *System of Transcendental Idealism* dealt with above. The problem was still so predominant in his later philosophy that he considered this philosophy a "system of freedom," which was to take up the struggle against Hegel's "system of necessity."

As was just noted, Schelling, in contrast to Hegel, was disturbed by the question of freedom only in regard to the freedom of finite, that is, human beings, which he viewed in relationship to divine being. In determining this relationship he was influenced at first by Spinoza, then by Böhme, and finally by the entire tradition of theosophic and cabbalistic thought (cf. below, p. 61). We have already seen that in the concept of history the problem of the relationship between freedom and necessity was posed in reference to "absolute identity," the Godhead, whose workings can never rationally be known, but only accepted through faith. The occurrence of the world and of man—history—could be explained in the end only by reference to the history of revelation, the occurrence of divine revelation. It may seem at first that history as universal history, which was supposed to guarantee individual freedom, had been conceived of only in a secular political-utopian way. It may seem that it referred to nothing other than the "successive realization of the One Ideal, the institution of a general legal constitution." But already in the later stages of the genesis described in the *System of Transcendental Idealism*, history was thought of in a religious and philosophical manner so that it became the "continuing revelation of the absolute in its gradual self-manifestation" (III, 603). This relationship to God, as seen from the human perspective, implied that man "in his history gives a continuing proof of the existence of God" (ibid.).

Thus, the following question arises: What is the meaning of the two

terms employed to determine the concept of history, freedom and necessity, if history is conceived of in reference to God as an occurrence of
revelation? The answer seems to be easy as far as one side of the
concept—necessity—is concerned. That which general, unphilosophical opinion regards as "fate" or "the laws of nature" and that passes for
"predetermination" in philosophy and religion is then endowed with
the sense of a "revelation of the divine plan of providence."

It is precisely from the standpoint of transcendental philosophy, however, that an insurmountable conceptual difficulty arises if necessity is
given such a meaning. We have seen that in transcendental philosophy
the constitution of a necessary occurrence was explained by means of an
"absolute synthesis" that proceeds unconsciously, a synthesis that
unites the contradictory free actions of intelligent beings in that which
is "objective" within them. Should this objectivity then be taken as
God's complete revelation, as a complete enactment of the providential
plan? That would mean that there would be nothing other than this
occurrence that unconsciously realizes itself, and this in turn would imply that conscious free activity does not exist. Yet this was precisely
what transcendental philosophy had set out to prove, that conscious,
free activity is the presupposition for the activity of unconscious constitution, and thus a presupposition for the absolute synthesis itself. If the
opposition between conscious and unconscious activity were negated,
then there could also be no absolute synthesis. Schelling argued here
without referring to transcendental philosophy: Does the supposition of
a perfect revelation not imply that the world is a perfect presentation of
God? And does this not mean that it cannot be other than it is? Nevertheless, he noted, there are changes, and these are instances of freedom.
Hence the world is not a perfect presentation of God; it is not the perfect revelation of divinity. Only by means of this premise can the other
side of the concept of history—freedom—be rescued. At an earlier
stage in transcendental philosophy, Schelling had demonstrated that
finite human freedom, the human will, presupposes an "absolute" freedom and an "absolute" will, even though within the bounds of finitude,
freedom and free will exist only in their internal appearance to us. As an
"internal appearance" we believe "that we are always internally free"
(602), that we have a free will that can choose among the various possibilities that present themselves to us. We believe in "voluntary choice"
[*Willkür*] in precisely this sense (cf. 573ff.). Schelling's concern here

was to rescue freedom "for the sake of appearance" (577, 603) and not to rescue absolute freedom and the absolute will that constitute the "play of freedom" for individuals and states. But how could internal freedom be rescued? The only way was to presuppose that the self-manifesting revelation of the absolute is never fully enacted; by supposing that—to speak transcendentally—the absolute synthesis never constitutes itself completely or—to speak empirically—that the plan of providence is never fully developed. The one side of the concept of history, necessity, may never be granted complete predominance. This implies that the other side, freedom, can still play an important part in the whole occurrence of history even though history is still considered to be an occurrence of revelation.

We have seen that teleo-logical necessity was bestowed with the character of an irresistible urge and constraint but that it was also said to be "sacred." What then was its relationship to finite human freedom? The answer turns out to be that in the *System of Transcendental Idealism* Schelling was not able to describe it in rigid conceptual terms. He merely sought to illustrate it through an expansive image. He wrote:

> We can think of history as a play in which everyone involved plays his role in complete freedom and according to his own fancy. A reasonable development in this confused play can be envisioned only if we conceive of there being *One Spirit* [*Ein Geist*] who acts as the playwright in all the individual players. Furthermore, we must think of the playwright in whom the individual actors are mere fragments (*disjecti membra poetae*), as already having harmonized the objective outcome of the whole with the free play of all individuals beforehand in such a way that something reasonable has to result. But in the end, if the playwright *existed* independently of his drama, then we would only be actors who performed what he has written. If he does not *exist* independently of us but rather reveals and successively manifests himself only in the very play of our freedom, so that he himself *would not exist* without this freedom, then we are poetic coauthors of the whole play and improvisors of the particular roles which we play. (602) (cf. below p. 82).

Let us take this vivid illustration of historical occurrence as a whole seriously and reflect on the meanings that necessity, on the one hand, and finite human freedom, on the other, are given within this framework. To begin with, the plan of providence itself, and not merely its revelation or presentation, is considered "incomplete." Even if this plan could be thought of as having One Spirit, or God, as its playwright, man is nevertheless defined not only as an actor who performs this plan or play, but also as a poetic "coauthor." If man is continually coauthoring the drama, then this means that the plan of divine providence is not yet completed. A contingency is thus introduced into self-fulfilling necessity. This is further reinforced by the fact that man as fellow actor in the playing out of the divine drama, the providential plan, is granted the status of a "self-improvisor of his own role." Man is given the possibility of performing in one way or another the drama he coauthors. But this does not go far enough. It is explicitly stated that not only the plan of providence, but also the poetic author himself, God, is "not independent" of the human play of freedom. The statement that God "would not exist at all" without this finite freedom follows as a necessary consequence from the preceding suppositions. Let us at this point disregard the thought, so enormous and frightful for traditional religion and philosophy, that God could become dependent on man: It suffices here to note that within the relationship of freedom and necessity it is freedom that is granted primacy.

What does this mean for Schelling's concept of history? Evidently we must make a distinction according to the period in which the revelation occurs. At the end of the second section of his *System of Transcendental Idealism*, the distinction is made between "three periods of revelation," which correspond to the division between fate, the plan of nature, and providence. Indeed, for Schelling, the whole occurrence shows itself as the event of a gradually self-revealing providence. According to the general understanding of his age, however, and we might include ours as well, history's lawfulness is attributed to the plan of nature, if no longer to fate. As noted, Schelling had earlier envisaged this plan's complete development in the genesis of a universal federation of nations, in the gradual self-development of mankind's legal constitution. If, however, the "only true" idea of history is now said to be the one in which the occurrence of an "incompletely self-revealing providence" (604) in a play presented for everyone, then we must take this as our point of departure and ask how the third historical period could be more precisely conceived of as the interplay between freedom and necessity. We have seen that Schelling determined the coexistence of freedom and necessity as a pre-established harmony (cf. above p. 8) founded in the "absolute identity" of a first principle or ground [*Grund*], that cannot be grasped in concepts. But what happens when human freedom is given a primacy such that it not only renders lawfulness—necessity—contingent, but the ground itself comes to be dependent on human freedom? Does that not imply the dissolution of the whole construction of a pre-established harmony that maintains two independent aspects in identity with one another, and sets them in a ground that is independent of the sphere of finitude and freedom? It does indeed. We thus come to the conclusion that Schelling was not able to grant human freedom a meaningful conceptual role in the teleological course of history without endangering the consistency of the whole framework that he had erected on the traditional foundation of a teleological subjectivity. It is here that we see why Schelling resorted to an image. In his later efforts to determine history, Schelling attempted to master this difficulty from various standpoints, but, for our particular purposes, we can reserve judgment as to whether or not he was successful in his efforts. Schelling was no doubt influenced by certain modern tendencies in his attempt to unite the primacy of human freedom with the absolute synthesis between freedom and necessity. But I am convinced that in any case his attempt in the *System of Transcendental Idealism* to unite them in an internally consistent concept did not succeed.

How consistent are contemporary conceptions that grant human freedom an even greater role than Schelling did and that nevertheless operate within a teleological framework, although the necessity for the realization of the development toward a *telos* is no longer guaranteed by divine providence? I shall attempt to answer this question by discussing the theory of history developed by Jürgen Habermas, as presented in his book *Knowledge and Human Interest* and in his inaugural lecture by the same name.

It may seem surprising that I contrast this theory of history to that of the young Schelling in view of the fact that in earlier works Habermas deals with the later Schelling's view of history,[8] and that the works dealt with here orient themselves toward Hegel, and not Schelling. Nevertheless, the methodological considerations involved in the selection of this particular theory of history were concerned solely with the constellation of unresolved contradictions between "freedom and necessity" as it has just been described. Habermas's theory renders the determining categories in the traditional foundation and problems implicit therein so distinctly visible that it is especially well suited as an illustration of the dilemma involved in many contemporary proposals.

V

EVEN AT first glance one is struck by the fact that Habermas's conception of history resembles Schelling's in that both of them considered history the process of the human species' self-constitution. Habermas seems to have shared Schelling's view that history is "only there" insofar as the "realization of One Ideal" through the species is concerned. For all appearances, this realization also assumes the form of a "progressive" movement toward a *telos*. This obvious agreement may then serve as justification for an examination as to whether and to what extent Habermas's notion of history is still conceived of on the basis of a traditional foundation of teleological subjectivity. If it is, then one should also consider the question as to whether and how the problem of the contradiction between "freedom and necessity" poses itself within this conception, and, if possible, how the problem is solved.

In order to characterize the position taken by Habermas as a whole, it should be noted that in his book *Knowledge and Human Interest* Habermas was primarily oriented toward Karl Marx. It seems at first that he adopted Marx's fundamental doctrines without any alterations: the mechanism of the development of the species' history is a "naturally formed" [*naturwüchsiger*] process, it fulfills itself in the natural reproduction of life. The human species, which in turn is natural and concrete, mediates itself through real labor with objective nature. This activity, directed toward objects and founded in the "history of nature," plays the decisive role in the species' self-production, which Marx in *Das Kapital* had defined as a "process of metabolism." In addition, it appears that Habermas adopted Marx's view that labor, on the one hand, is posited in natural history, and, on the other, is socially organized. He furthermore accepted the thesis that the power of disposition over external nature, which immediately confronts man and is processed through labor, is dependent on the particular level of the productive forces. And finally, Habermas seems to have shared Marx's view concerning the central role of the category of class conflicts: He, too, was convinced that the production of the social forms of cooperation and the division of labor, as well as the acquisition of socially produced goods, are the result of class conflict.

Has Habermas's orientation on Marx then led him to overcome the traditional guiding thought expressed in the term "*logos*?" That this is not the case is indicated already by the very fact that he operatively employed many fundamental concepts that have their origin in the philosophy of *logos*. Habermas undertook to represent many of Marx's aforementioned positions as if they had been thought of not only "epistemologically,"[9] but also "transcendentally" (39, 28; 57, 41). He even characterized the economic mechanism of the species' historical development as an element in the "history of transcendental consciousness" (58, 41; 65, 48). Thus he declared that Marx's characterization of man as an objective being was not meant anthropologically but rather epistemologically (38, 26). The "objective activity" of which Marx spoke had the specific meaning of a "constitution of objects;" Marx understood it as a "transcendental achievement," Habermas said, since it corresponds to the constitution of a world in which reality is subjected to the conditions for the objectivity of possible objects. Labor and class conflict in particular are subsumed under the concept of "synthesis," a concept that is admittedly one of the most important terms in transcendental logic.

In introducing these traditional logical determinations, Habermas, of course, repeatedly emphasized that he wished them to be understood "at once" "empirically" and "materialistically," or "naturalistically." Knowing and acting have a "basis in nature."[10] The subject of world constitution is not "transcendental consciousness in general" but rather the "concrete human species which reproduces its life under natural conditions."[11] The species is the contingent product of its and of nature's history; and the "synthesis" of the labor process is "*to the same extent* an empirical and a transcendental achievement of a species that produces itself in history" (43, 31). This synthesis does not produce an "absolute synthesis of mind and nature;" the unity to be envisaged here is rather "imposed upon nature by the subject, so to speak" (45, 32).

In spite of his efforts to alter the original meanings of these concepts derived from the traditional foundation, Habermas's thought appears to remain thoroughly caught up in them.[12] This is confirmed above all by the fact that, in complete contrast with Marx, he granted spirit or mind, *Geist*,[13] almost the same power given it traditionally. Through the mind's ability to reflect the "cultural break with nature" (107) and to "become aware of the transcendental boundaries of possible conceptions of the world" (100), "a part of nature gains autonomy in nature through us" (ibid.). The mind is capable of becoming aware of its basis in nature. This is the crucial point in his entire doctrine: the mind has the power of reflection.[14] Habermas's conviction concerning the power of *logos* forced him to "revise" Marx. According to Habermas, Marx had not admitted the validity of reflection as such, although he had employed it in his "critique of ideology." In principle, however, Marx "deceived himself into ignoring reflection"; it "escapes him" as the form of historical movement, especially in his conception of class conflict.[15] Marx ignored the "dimension of self-reflection," and for this reason he falsely determined the science of man in analogy to natural science.[16] Habermas, however, contended that the species' process of self-production is a process of oppression and self-liberation and that for this very reason it must be conceived of at the same time as the pathway of a process toward "social cultivation" [*Bildung*] by means of an appropriate category here: reflection. "The course of the process of social cultivation, by contrast, is marked not by new technologies, but by stages of reflection . . ." (76, 55). Accordingly, the concept of "synthesis" that Habermas introduced must refer not only to self-production through labor, but also to self-production as improvement through social practice, and that means through reflection and self-reflection.

In the traditional philosophy of *logos*, particularly during the age of Enlightenment, the view obtained that conduct and hence voluntary action can and must be rational. Furthermore, Kant had demonstrated in the *Foundations for a Metaphysics of Morals*[17] that freedom must be presupposed as a "property of the will of all rational beings." Habermas seldom made use of the traditional category of freedom. Nevertheless, as far as the issue at hand is concerned, social action as the propagation of enlightening reflection is a form of rational freedom. And from the point of view of Schelling's *System of Transcendental Idealism*, it already progressed beyond mere "voluntary choice" [*Willkür*] that chooses between various possibilities according to its own advantage. We have seen in Schelling's case that freedom as voluntary choice, such as it appears in the "selfish desires of individuals and states," did not lead to social action. Thus the decisive question for Schelling in his philosophy of history was how, in spite of voluntary choice on the part of individuals and nations, all endeavors could still be brought together under a goal of the species as a whole. As we have seen, Schelling attempted to solve this problem, on the one hand, by means of the conception of an unconsciously self-fulfilling transcendental synthesis, and, on the other hand, by including divine providence and the occurrence of revelation in the transcendental genesis as the guarantee for the necessity of the fulfillment of *telos*.

Habermas, however, seems to have seen no problem in the fact that in spite of individuals' selfish desires, "social" action comes about at the level of the species. He also seems to have found just as little difficulty in the fact that this action unites itself under one goal in opposition to all individuals' endeavors. Is our supposition thus confirmed that his theory of history is a teleological conception? In fact, in his inaugural lecture an "idea" [*Idee*] in the sense of an "ideal" is spoken of—an "idea" that the "human species" must "realize."[18] For Habermas, this idea, the "only one which we are capable of according to the philosophical tradition" (163), is "mature responsibility" [*Mündigkeit*]. The human species has to "realize" this "responsibility" by means of a "progression" toward it (164). It would be fully realized in an "emancipated society" (ibid.), in which "communication is raised to the level of a dialogue, free of domination, between one and all" (ibid.). An emancipated society that has realized the domination—free dialogue among all of its members is the final stage of a "successful life" that each society "imagines" (ibid.).[19] These statements are unequivocal verification that Habermas's theory is "teleological."

In accordance with Habermas's own presuppositions of the species' "social practice" as a "rational freedom" one might then ask: Had he conceived of a "necessity" governing the course by which the species approaches its goal, and had the contradiction between this necessity and the freedom of social action emerged for him as a problem? If it had, how had he tried to solve it?

At this point we have to recall the development, the first indications of which we recognized so graphically in that image in which the young Schelling, under the domination of religious ideas, granted finite human freedom such a broad latitude. This development toward an emphasis on human freedom has continued, though in a new direction. It was Feuerbach, Marx, and his successors, as well as the "philosophers of life," Nietzsche and Dilthey, contemporary philosophers of anthropology such as Scheler, existentialists such as Sartre, and many other contemporary philosophers, especially Heidegger and Löwith, who have, as we mentioned, called into question the theological presuppositions of a philosophy of history. Furthermore, empiricism and analytic and linguistic trends have mounted attacks on every sort of speculatively presented, logically constructed philosophy. These and other factors have led to the conviction dominant today that man "makes his history" all by himself. The dictum of Vico's *Scienza Nuova*, "*verum et factum convertuntur*," has long since been interpreted in this sense. It is obvious that Habermas's stance is completely within the compass of the modern view that history can be produced even though he was aware that this view itself has historical origins, as indicated especially in his essays in *Theory and Practice*. For this reason alone, the problem of a teleological history of the species and the problem of freedom and necessity within the framework of history must pose themselves differently for him than for Schelling. *Telos* is no longer an *eschaton* in the history of salvation; the "emancipated" society is its "secularized" form. Habermas could not then conceive of the necessity of the teleological course of history as being guaranteed by divine providence. This does not mean, however, that no "necessity" at all can be postulated in a concept of history that would determine why the *telos* will be reached. One can only suppose a *telos* under the presupposition that it is possible to prove that the species can realize or at least approach this *telos*. If the intention of the theory of history presented in *Knowledge and Human Interest* is to secure reflection, then we can see that the species' fulfillment of freedom is supposed to be the proper instrument for this goal. Nonetheless, we must inquire whether Habermas had determined "reflection" to be that power that, along with the pressure of the "forces of production,"[20] acts as the "motor" in history and guides it to its *telos*.[21]

VI

THE DETERMINATION "reflection" has its origins in the philosophy of *logos*, of reason, which established itself in the modern age as the philosophy of subjectivity. "Re-flection," the form of a self turning toward itself, Descartes's *cogito me cogitare*, allowed the essence of an ego that can be characterized as a self, the essence of a *res cogitans*, to emerge for the first time. In the experiment of doubting, this self maintains its independence from the givenness of immediately presented "reality." The ego possesses the unfathomable power to direct itself toward everything possible through representations [*Vorstellungen*]. By means of a *cohibere assensionem*, it can suspend the immediacy of the merely sensual reference to being as a "reality" that is given sensually, and can thus persevere in a self-established reflective relation toward itself.

In the course of subsequent history this power was raised to a "principle." For Kant reflection was above all the method for the discovery of the transcendental subject as this principle. Among the sources of knowledge, transcendental investigation discovered this principle to be the condition for the possibility of all theoretical knowledge; with reference to the good, it was transcendental subjectivity in the form of the rational will's power to establish moral laws that was discovered as the foundation for all moral action. For Fichte, reflection was not only a method, but it also constituted the essence of the ego conceived as a principle. Hegel, too, saw it in this manner, specifically under the form of "absolute reflection" that immersed itself in the dialectical movement of the determinations of thought. In addition to this sort of reflection, however, Hegel discerned two others: the methodological reflection that was presented in the *Phenomenology* as "phenomenological" and works its way up to "absolute reflection" together with a second type of reflection, the reflection of "mere understanding" [*verständige Reflexion*], which is employed by "natural consciousness."

It is especially important to note that, instead of presenting a determination of reflection on his own, Habermas took two concepts of reflection from Hegel's *Phenomenology* as his model in *Knowledge and Human Interest*. This book, which sets out to present a social theory in the form of a "reconstruction of recent positivism's prehistory" (9, *vii*), begins with an interpretation of Hegel's *Phenomenology* that remains decisive for his entire line of thought. Habermas expressly stated: "Social theory thus remains caught up in the framework of the *Phenomenology*." [22] This implies the following: If we want to find out what reflection means in Habermas's work and whether—as the fulfillment of freedom—it also has the power to guarantee teleological necessity, then we must investigate how and why his theory of history attempts to model itself on that "method" that in the *Phenomenology* was indeed capable of bringing "history" to its *telos*.

In investigating this question, we should pay special attention to one point in particular:[23] In Hegel's view, the "method," the *Phenomenology's* law of movement that leads to the *telos*, is prescribed entirely by his point of departure in the nature of universal self-consciousness as concept. The decisive statement in the introduction to the *Phenomenology* is that consciousness is "for itself its concept."[24] For this reason alone could "phenomenological reflection" set out to transform the mere reflection of understanding into something higher: the reflection of understanding was seen to be bogged down by fixations and dichotomy in its basic determinations at first, but by means of an exhibition [*Darstellung*] phenomenological consciousness is said to be capable of demonstrating a "history of cultivation or education" [*Bildungsgeschichte*]. And since the reflection of mere understanding could subsequently retrace this history, this history must lead to the *telos* whose "time has come," "absolute reflection." Only by taking the nature of self-consciousness as concept for its point of departure was it possible for phenomenological reflection to "gather" [*versammeln*] (ibid., 556, 485) the forms of knowledge lying in this concept together in a history of experience such that its "result" necessarily leads to its "final form,"— "absolute knowledge." Only those forms of knowledge that lay in the concept and accompanied phenomenological reflection in its presentation along the pathway of experience were given the name "phenomenological knowledge" [*erscheinendes Wissen*] by Hegel, who carefully distinguished such knowledge, as a qualified form of "natural consciousness," from natural consciousness itself, which was considered contingently historical.[25]

From the very outset, his orientation toward Marx precluded Habermas from interpreting his own theory of history as a history of cultivation that has absolute knowledge as its goal.[26] It is simply impossible that Hegel's point of departure in the nature of general self-consciousness as concept could serve the same purpose in Habermas's theory of history. Nevertheless, it should still be noted that Habermas obviously constructed his theory of history in *Knowledge and Human Interest* with conscious reference to the *Phenomenology*. Just as Hegel distinguished between phenomenological reflection and that of consciousness that is "involved in the process of experience," and just as the latter is tied to the former, so too did Habermas distinguish between the reflection of the social theorist and the species' "process of reflection as a whole."[27] The former sort of reflection is in turn tied to the latter, whereby the issue in this "reconstruction" is every bit as much a "history of cultivation" as the Hegelian *Phenomenology* purports to be. Habermas's reconstructed history of cultivation, however, is intended as a history of the conflicts inherent in "class consciousness" that lead to the *telos* of an "emancipated society." "Class-consciousness" is by no means an "idealistically" conceived form of "phenomenal knowledge," but is rather materialistic (83, *61*) and thus contingently historical. Habermas himself determined it as a consciousness that has cultivated itself "on the basis of the objectivized forms in which external nature is appropriated." It is contingent in every way. Why did he nevertheless term this contingently historical "natural" consciousness "phenomenal" without referring back to that fundamental distinction in the *Phenomenology*? Here we see that Habermas's intention was to correct the one-sided materialistic and economic interpretation of the species' history presented in "Technology and Science as Ideology." Furthermore, it becomes plain that Habermas sought to utilize the *Phenomenology's* method as a "motor" for a "further process of determination" that would necessarily lead history to its *telos*.

The reflection of "phenomenal knowledge" is driven restlessly by the power of thought that is inherent in phenomenal knowledge "in itself" due to its nature as a concept. It is driven to overcome itself and all limitations alien to the concept, and to conduct itself "sceptically" toward all natural presuppositions alien to the concept.[28] It is driven to pursue this self-liberation until it finds its way back to its true nature, its nature as concept (75)—until it becomes "in and for itself" [*an und für sich*] (see below, p. 54). If it were not "in itself" concept, this movement of reflection would not be induced. But how is reflection supposed to come about in the case of contingent class-consciousness? How is the transition made from the materialistic basis to thought? Habermas assured us that the reflection of class-consciousness is "induced [*ausgelöst*] due to the growing potential to regulate the processes in nature which are objectified by labor."[29] He did not show, however, how such an "inducement" occurs.[30] According to the *Phenomenology's* method,[31] further progress in the determination of "phenomenal knowledge" results from the fact that consciousness compares its changing shapes to a standard that lies in its own nature as concept.[32] It examines whether each particular instance of knowledge is "true" and whether each particular content corresponds to consciousness as "true." By means of this examining movement consciousness can proceed on its own from one object of experience to a new one. Class-consciousness, which does not have its origins in the nature of self-consciousness as concept, is incapable of such self-examination and self-correction. Since he proceeded from the supposition that even here the issue is that of a history of cultivation that passes through "stages of reflection,"[33] however, Habermas still declared that "phenomenal class-consciousness" can recognize "existing untruth" in the "discrepancy between institutionally demanded and objectively necessary repression." He claimed that it has the critical ability to "unmask each existing form of life as an abstraction and thereby revolutionize it" (pp. 83, 61ff.). But, Habermas did not prove this either, he only attempted to make it plausible by referring to Hegel's "method."

Perhaps Habermas's intention was less to determine the species' reflection than to determine the "cognitive consciousness" of the historical theorist so that his consciousness would have the power to approach the species' *telos*. But he did not systematically determine this reflection either. Instead, its role is compared to the role that the phenomenologist plays in Hegel's *Phenomenology*. Habermas's view of this role is correct insofar as he stressed that the phenomenologist is "involved" (84, 61) in the process of the cultivation of consciousness and insofar as he emphasized this dependence in order to explain how the phenomenologist "recognizes himself as the result of the history of phenomenal class-consciousness" (ibid.). On the other hand, it must still be recalled that the *Phenomenology* is an "emerging and phenomenal science" only because absolute knowledge has autonomously "separated itself into powers" [*sich depotenziert*] in order to fulfill the task characterized above. It is quite simply impossible for the historical theoretician to play the same role as the phenomenologist in the *Phenomenology of Spirit*. The phenomenologist is able to recognize a "chain" that has constituted itself behind "phenomenal knowledge's" back—a chain that lends the teleological process exactly that "necessity" with which it develops up to the last shape in the pathway to cultivation. This chain, however, is constituted only through the examining movement of "phenomenal knowledge." "Phenomenal knowledge" experiences at every stage of the way that it does not correspond to its particular object, that it is a "nothing." It is thus prompted to pass over to the new object that—this is precisely what the phenomenologist recognizes—contains the experience of the previous object, and thus it is determined by its insight into the nothingness of the previous object.[34] The theorist of history has as his object "class-consciousness" that, because it lacks a conceptual nature, does not undergo an examining movement and thus does not experience the "nothingness" of its previous object. There is then no chain of "determinate nothingness" [*bestimmte Nichts*] for him, and it is impossible for the role of the critical theorist of history to coincide with that of the phenomenologist.

The decisive reason why neither the consciousness of phenomenal knowledge nor that of the phenomenologist can coincide with that of the historical theorist is above all the fact that only the former are both guided by "categories" (ibid.). As opposed to the categories in the *Logic*, these categories appear in the *Phenomenology* "for consciousness" as "shapes of consciousness." They are "moments" that constitute the "standard" for the self-examination of phenomenal knowledge (see below p. 54), a standard that is "present in consciousness itself" (75, 57; 72, 54). The fact that the categories ultimately guide this whole movement in the *Phenomenology* explains the primacy of "necessity," by means of which Hegel resolved the contradiction between "freedom and necessity" in this "philosophy of history." For the reasons mentioned above, this necessity is "divine" for him (see above p. 13). No further proof is required to ascertain that neither the reflection of the theorist of history nor that of class-consciousness is comprehended as being guided by "divine" thoughts. It can be clearly seen at this point that the *Phenomenology*'s method, resting as it does on the primacy of necessity, is not at all suited to proving that reflection in the form of social practice possesses the power to act as the exclusive guarantor for the *telos* of an emancipated society.

I shall not here deal with the question as to whether or not in the course of his investigations Habermas himself realized how problematic his attempt to simulate the method of the *Phenomenology* really was.[35] In any case, in the last chapter of his book Habermas no longer tried to determine reflection on the basis of Hegel, but on the basis of the later Freud's writings on a theory of culture. By reading Freud together with Marx, Habermas declared that Freud had developed metapsychological theories in which institutions recognized as the powers that legitimize domination, as the powers from which "ideologically captive consciousness can be liberated through self-reflection if a new potential in the domination of nature makes previous legitimations implausible."[36] Freud is also supposed to have clearly stated the direction of the species' history: "The development of the productive forces demonstrates at every stage anew the objective possibilities of relaxing the social framework and of replacing the affective foundations of cultural obedience with rational ones" (344, 283). Here, too, just as in the essay on technology, which Habermas published at the same time, it is the economic foundations that set free the "objective possibilities" of history's further course and that thus determine the particular direction of historical development. The "goal" of history, according to a quotation from Freud, is "the rational foundation of cultural prescriptions." Habermas attempted to determine "social reflection" here after the model of a neurotic patient's reflective activity, but still to retain the notion of "stages of reflection" (which has its origins in Hegel's history of cultivation) as well as the Marxist notion of class-conflict. He transposed the interaction between the therapist and the patient, who is motivated by the desire to recover, into the strategic conflicts of class struggle. Self-reflection is now said to be capable of discerning all that which obscurely determines us in the politically and institutionally organized world. It is said to be capable of changing the real political conditions by inducing political interaction.

Ever since the age of Greek philosophy, tradition has proceeded from the assumption that the universe is fundamentally intelligible and that human reason is designed to realize this intelligibility of the universe. Traditionally, the notion of "enlightenment" has also involved the possibility of changing the state of society. But does this not imply that Habermas's attempt to orient social reflection on the model of a neurotic patient is an extension of the power of reflection as it has been traditionally viewed? The reflective experience of "pseudo-praxis" is, at least in the case of the patient, "tied to the act of overcoming pseudo-natural compulsions" (401). Did Habermas think that this model could be carried over and applied to large groups so that the enlightenment of social consciousness, at the very moment it becomes internalized, not only supersedes "false consciousness" but also eliminates repression and the compulsion that accompanies it?[37] Instead of extending the power of reflection, and thus of freedom, so that they could be the "motor" of his teleological construction of history, Habermas shared the reservations concerning the power of reflection that Freud expressed in his theoretical considerations of culture. In the chapter on Freud in *Knowledge and Human Interest*, the logic in the movement of reflection directed against repression and ideology is said to be a mere "logic of trial and error" (344, 284). There is said to be no "promise" at all that the development of the productive forces will ever bring about the objective possibility of a complete liberation of the institutional framework from repression.

The actions of enlightenment can only be understood as an attempt to "test the bounds for the possibility of realizing the utopian context in the cultural tradition under given conditions" (ibid.). Such a cautiously determined freedom in the form of social reflection can no longer be said to be capable of guaranteeing teleological necessity in the manner that would be required for the general conception of a theory of history.

We thus come to the following conclusion: In his efforts to resolve the contradiction between freedom and necessity on the basis of the traditional foundation, Schelling reached the limits of what can be grasped in strictly logical concepts when he tried to grant human freedom a broader role than divine providence. Habermas's thought, however, is just as much based on a traditional notion of teleological subjectivity. His secularized version of a final goal in the history of the species led him to construct his theory of history teleologically. His belief in the power of enlightenment and social practice explains his attempt at the same time to rescue reflection, and thus to rescue a form of that which is termed reason and freedom in the tradition. This attempt, however, entangled him in the traditional contradiction between freedom and necessity, although he did not consciously confront the problem of this contradiction. A certain inconsistency becomes apparent: For a theory of history that does not refer to God, human freedom or reflection by means of social action is the only possible guarantee that a certain *telos* will of necessity be fulfilled. It must provide for the necessity in history. But under the influence of certain modern trends of thought (especially Freud), Habermas determined human freedom or reflection by means of social action so weakly that it cannot possibly provide for the necessity of a *telos*. This teleological theory of history thus lacks inner consistency. In accordance with the Marxist maxim that philosophy has been overcome [*aufgehoben*],[38] Habermas no longer accepted the traditional philosophical task of "thinking categories"; he employed them "operatively" without an awareness of the context in which they belong. This context, however, would provide the only possible basis for the decision as to whether and how they presuppose one another.

Could it be that Habermas in the meanwhile came to recognize this? In the discussion of his theory of history, we have neglected the fact that for him emancipation implied the possibility of rationally making oneself understood through communication free of repression.[39] This idea, which in his inaugural address he had already derived from the structure of language, plays an important role in many of his later endeavors. Hence, Habermas reiterated in the preface to "Theory and Praxis" (23–24) that "mature responsibility" [*Mündigkeit*] is the only idea "which we are capable of . . . according to the tradition," and that "in one's very first sentence . . . the intention of a general consensus without compulsion [is] expressed unmistakably." In his most recent publications concerning a theory of communicative competence, he tried to determine this idea—which as a form of social life is the goal for the species' emancipatory development—more closely by means of a universal pragmatics. Referring to Searle's theory of speech acts, Habermas constructed an ideal situation for dialogue in which an ideal distribution of the speakers' roles is pre-established. This construction is no mere fiction for him; it is rather a "contrafactual anticipation" that every speaker and listener must intend if communication is to be at all possible, and that can thus be derived quasi-analytically from the "metacommunication" inherent in every dialogue.

Habermas attempted to grasp traditional categories such as truth, freedom, and justice in a new way through a theory of language,[40] but that attempt does not imply that any progress has been made in relation to the difficulties that we have demonstrated in his theory of history. For, in the first place, universal pragmatics is concerned only with a "logic" of speech, with performances that result from the status of universals (or the relationship of performatory phrases to propositional ones). It concerns itself with the rules for speech competence that are determined without any reference to life-worlds [*Lebenswelten*] of a historical kind. The rules for communication processes are completely ahistorical and do not contain a "motor" for emancipatory progress. Furthermore, the theory of contrafactual anticipation does not constitute a solution to the problem concerning the philosophy of history. Although this anticipation is also supposed to have constitutive significance for factually existent communication, it is no more than an imperative with reference to the human species' future development. This might lead to the conclusion that Habermas had clearly turned away from teleological thought once and for all. This is refuted, however, by the fact that his philosophy of history still remains oriented toward Hegel and Marx. His *Grundannahmen einer historischen Materialismus* (285ff.) [*Basic Suppositions for Historical Materialism*] demonstrates that progress and necessity are still the decisive categories in his interpretation of history; and in his recent book[41] he outlined the much more extensive project of a "logic of moral systems" or "world views" [*Weltbilder*], projects that transcend the economic realm. Even if there were still a logic immanent in the development of history today, it still remains an open question what the motor of this development would be in the future, and what kind of necessity history would possess in its future course. Habermas's notion of "a contrafactual anticipation" is interesting, even though—as he himself admitted—it is "unclear." But in spite of this notion, his most recent studies have still failed to resolve the dilemma in his philosophy of history. For this dilemma is prompted by the implicitly teleological conception that he himself would like to overcome.

2

The Task and Method of Philosophy in Schelling's *System of Transcendental Idealism* and in Hegel's *Phenomenology of Spirit*

I N THIS STUDY I intend to relate certain aspects of Schelling's Transcendental System of 1800 to Hegel's *Phenomenology* of 1807, two works that were composed within a very few years of each other. How can such an attempt be justified in view of the fact that we today are so intensely aware of the difficulties involved in tracing the historical development of these two philosophers' thought? We are indebted to the work in philosophical reconstruction done by Otto Pöggeler and Heinz Kimmerle at the Hegel Archives in Bochum for our knowledge that, especially during the period from Jena until the composition of the *Phenomenology*, Hegel's conception of the system was modified several times. It is also evident that Schelling's philosophizing was subject to continual transformation from 1800 until 1807. But nonetheless, surely no one will dispute that in addition to the connections involved in the historical development of certain philosophers' thought, there can be a connection between different philosophical works that results from their common issue. This is especially true when different works by different authors, although composed at different times, are based on the same principle, or when on account of a common view concerning the "task of philosophy," different works merely represent varying attempts to fulfill the same task.

I therefore derive the justification for this study from the fact that, although in a modified version, Hegel's *Phenomenology* proceeded from the same principle as Schelling's Transcendental System. Furthermore, the *Phenomenology* still understood the "task of philosophy" as Schelling had understood it in 1800. One year later in his *Differenzschrift* [*The Difference between Fichte's and Schelling's Systems of Philosophy*] Hegel declared it to be a view they held in common. Without pursuing a question that has interested me for more than a decade,[1] and has still never been fully answered—the question as to whether and to what extent Hegel's and Schelling's positions in the *Differenzschrift* still corresponded—one can ascertain that Schelling surely would have consented to the following Hegelian determination of the "task of philosophy": Philosophy must "overcome" [*aufheben*][2] the traditional oppositions such as reason and sensuality, intelligence and nature. (In the *Ideen* of 1797 Schelling had spoken of the "division" [*Trennung*] between consciousness and the forces in nature.) Philosophy has to overcome this "dichotomy" [*Entzweiung*] in knowledge, which the philosophy of reflection [*Reflexionsphilosophie*] during Hegel's era is said to have rigidified into the opposition between "absolute subjectivity" and "absolute objectivity." This "overcoming" was to be achieved by developing the principle of modern philosophy that had found its culmination in Fichte's systematic Idealism. "Fichte's philosophy is . . . a genuine product of speculation," wrote Hegel in the *Differenzschrift* (I, 272).

In the first section of this study, I intend to show how Schelling's Transcendental System can be understood as an attempt to fulfill the task of overcoming this fundamental dichotomy, even though this system constituted only one part of Schelling's whole system at that time. This will be the guiding consideration in my analysis of Schelling's conception and composition of this system. This conception will not be explained by referring to Fichte, as one might expect at first, nor primarily by reference to Schelling's later reflections on this work. Instead I intend to 'stick to the text'. This cannot, of course, be achieved by merely interpreting various passages of that text. Rather, in the following studies I shall concentrate on the meaning of Schelling's basic idea, for we must be able to see how and why systematic philosophizing was *possible* for him on the basis of this idea. The point of my question might be formulated in the following manner: "Is systematic philosophy still possible today?" As opposed to numerous other responses to this question, which have been offered during this and the last century, a new answer to this question can be prepared within the framework of a theme taken from the history of philosophy only by exposing the basic notions of various idealistic systems, and then inquiring as to whether and how they entailed the necessity for systematic philosophizing.

My second step will be to discuss certain aspects of the method presented in Schelling's Transcendental System. I am convinced that this can be especially helpful in the clarification of the method in Hegel's *Phenomenology*. Such clarification is still necessary, to no small degree on account of the fact that representatives of various philosophical movements current today still discern in Hegel's method either a justification for, or opposition to their own efforts.

I

HEGEL STATES in the *Differenzschrift*: "The absolute principle, the only real ground and solid standpoint for philosophy in Fichte's and Schelling's philosophy is intellectual intuition—expressed in terms of reflection: the identity of subject and object" (I, 271).

Through this identification of the "absolute principle" and "intellectual intuition," Hegel has abstracted from the agent of intuition, from the philosopher who has freed himself from all object-related representations, and has performed the intellectual intuition. Schelling himself had abstracted from the subjective act only for purely theoretical philosophy, for the philosophy of nature. In his Transcendental System he identified intellectual intuition, which is freely generated, with the ego (III, 369–70). In this sort of intellectual intuition, the producing and the intuiting self are one with and the same as that which is produced and intuited. Intellectual intuition here is seen as the ego that withdraws from the succession of time into the immanent realm (I, 318); it is comprehended as the pure atemporal activity (374–75, 396–97) of a self-production that becomes an object only "for itself." This accomplishment, not limited by any object to be found in the world and completely void of presuppositions, this "non-objectivity" (350–51, cf. 600–601), is considered something absolutely free (cf. 376), detached from all beings, and sustaining itself in its own Being. As such it is the one and only point where subjectivity and objectivity are completely and immediately one and the same: It is that "which is absolutely identical," [*das absolut Identische*] which, according to the quotation from Hegel's *Differenzschrift* mentioned above, is "the identity of subject and object for reflection." In its complete self-sufficiency, it can never be an object for knowledge; it can only be the object of an "eternal pre-supposition in acting, i.e. of faith" (600–601). Absolute identity is the "principle" for all knowledge and for all conscious action, which are themselves split up into subject and object. It is a principle that ex-presses an unconditionally posited axiom that has only one condition: itself. Precisely because form and content mutually presuppose each other in this axiom, this principle is said to be capable of providing a foundation for the whole content of science, and above all for the form of its unity, for the systematic character of "philosophy as science" (cf. 359–60 and I, 89; 92; 69).

But why does Schelling identify this principle with intellectual intui-tion? In this respect he is less a successor of Fichte than of Spinoza, and here one can discern the influence of mysticism and of Hölderlin. It is "intellectual" because here in contrast to "sensuous" intuition, the very *intuiting itself* is distinct from that which is intuited (III, 369-70): Such intuiting is not restricted in its freedom by that which it intuits. Rather, it is a realization of the spontaneity of the intellect, of reason: It is the accomplishment of reason's freedom as "absolutely free knowing" (368-69). Even though intellectual intuition does not create things out of nothing like the *intellectus divinus*, it does generate itself as that ego which freely produces all of their determinations. Schelling de-scribed this intuition as "intellectual" because it is reason in its freedom and because it is spontaneous in its own self-construction. Thus he wrote: "The beginning and the end of this philosophy [is] *freedom*, that which is absolutely indemonstrable, which proves itself through itself alone" (376).

It seems to me that contemporary philosophy should be reminded over and over again of the following: Hegel, Fichte, and the young Schelling (who is our sole concern here) were convinced that in finite consciousness there is a dimension that, like creation from nothing, is an original, self-generating dimension not limited by objects (368-69), and in this sense a *free* dimension. They held this dimension to be the principle on the basis of which one could fulfill Kant's expectation of "philosophy as science."

But why was this spontaneity for Schelling not the spontaneity of the reflection of understanding or rational reflection, a term one can use in reference to Schelling if it is understood as "speculation?"[3] Why was it rather the spontaneity of "intuition?" The uniqueness of Schelling's

Idealism with its genetic procedure lies in the fact that it views the spontaneity of reason as prereflective,[4] and thus seeks to discover its workings in the region "beyond common consciousness" (527-28; X, 93). These workings of reason are themselves preconscious—we become conscious of them only in their results. And this is the source of the pertinence and fascination of his attempt for us today as we seek more now than ever to understand the way in which our comprehension and action "happen to us," to understand their "passivity." In his *Ideen zu einer Philosophie der Natur* [*Ideas Concerning a Philosophy of Nature*] (1797), Schelling had already praised the faculty of intuition insofar as it is consciously fulfilled, as the faculty "supreme in the human spirit" (II, 222). This supremacy lies in the fact that it is able to make the activities intuitable that produce the representations of the objective world and, in particular, material representations. In the Transcendental System he designated those preconscious activities, which make freely acting self-consciousness possible, as "intuitions," as "an intuiting" or as "that which intuits," insofar as these activities produce in an original and immediate way the "objectivity" of the "subject— object," i.e., the unconscious lawfulness of intelligence in its process of becoming conscious (cf. e.g. III, 382-83ff., 408-9, 410ff., 505-6, 567-68, 597-98ff., 631-32). Here one must not understand this broad concept of intuition as cognitive, analytic reflection, or as a speculative reflection that mediates the related extremes with each other through negative self-reference. It is in this vein that Schelling emphatically declared in the *System of Transcendental Idealism*: "Our whole philosophy (rests) on the standpoint of intuition, not on that of reflection . . ." (455-56).

Until now we have dealt only with the principle of Schelling's system and not with the conception of this system. It is obvious that a whole system of propositions can be developed only if one does not limit oneself to the positing of the principle, i.e., if one does not remain on the level of the "fundamental proposition" [*Grund-satz*]. Rather one must also demonstrate that this principle is the foundation for the whole realm of empirical knowledge and cognate activity. It is necessary to reconstruct how and why this principle—the spontaneity of reason— makes all knowledge possible through its lawlike constructive activity. One must show how, in the workings of the unity of subject-object, harmony emerges between the sum-total of all unconscious objects, i.e.

"nature" in this broad sense that includes the intellectual and historical world, and the sum-total of all conscious subjects (cf. 335ff.). If such a demonstration were successful, then not only would Fichte's Subjective Idealism have been overcome, but also the dichotomy between absolute subjectivity and absolute objectivity. The task of philosophy would have been fulfilled.

In reference to the conception of this system, however, one must inquire whether its point of departure, the principle of intellectual intuition as the fulfillment of freedom, entails any *necessity* for the fact that the system *must* be constructed as a positing that serves as the foundation for the whole of what can be known. Schelling had already inquired into the necessity for proceeding from an absolute into the realm of finitude in his earlier works. There, he had attempted to distinguish between Fichte's absolute position of an unlimitable ego, which posits itself as an absolute beyond which one cannot proceed, and self-positing in the sense of a self-consciousness, in which everything else is posited and which can only be transcendentally explained by simultaneously thinking of the opposite positing, the "opposition" of a "nonego" [*ein Nicht-Ich*].

The difficulties[5] involved in Schelling's early attempts also appear to predominate, though to a lesser extent, in the *System of Transcendental Idealism*. I shall not explore this problem here because my intention is to show that, in accordance with Schelling's basic notion of "intuition" as "self-intuition," his system provides a foundation for the necessity involved in the development of the absolute principle into finitude. Hegel's view, as expressed in his famous critique of Schelling in the *Phenomenology*, was that it lies in the very nature of intuition to "go no further than just where it begins" (*PhG* 18, 8). This view appears to me to be refuted by the fact that for Schelling the meaning involved in the terms "intuition" and "self-intuition" not only entailed a necessity to proceed to "finitude," but also to proceed to a systematic presentation of "everything that can be known" as well. Therefore, the conception and composition of this system can be best illustrated by clarifying what is entailed in this meaning.

For the systematic conception and composition of the Transcendental System, the most important aspect contained in the meaning of intuition as self-intuition is an aspect that Schelling took for granted, namely that intuition is a faculty that "produces by means of a primordial force, from within itself" (III, 427–28). This view is an expression of a concept of nature modeled on the Spinozistic *natura naturans*, which views nature as an all-encompassing creative process that is thus also the foundation for knowledge. Self-intuition is "productive" in this sense. The compulsion to correspond to this essence provides a very convincing explanation, first of all, for the fact that intuition discloses itself in a series of steps in which it brings forth "powers" [*Potenzen*] within itself; and second, for the fact that intuition is fulfilled in a form that is the expression of utmost productivity. Schelling states accordingly: "It is the poetic faculty that is called original intuition in the first power; and, conversely, that which we call the poetic faculty in the highest power" (625). If one clearly sees the connotation attached to "productivity," which Schelling saw in the term "self-intuition," then one can understand why the system's form of fulfillment is aesthetic and why the work of art is its product. The following retrospective insight, recorded by Schelling in the "Allgemeine Anmerkungen zu dem ganzen System" [General Remarks Concerning the System as a Whole], confirms that the necessity for the construction of a system lay in the meaning of self-intuition conceived of in this way: "the entire inner cohesiveness of Transcendental Philosophy rests upon self-intuition's continually raising itself to a power, from the first power in self-consciousness up until the highest, the aesthetic power" (630ff.).

Even more fundamental, however, was Schelling's conviction that the meaning of self-intuition implies that the movement of this genesis is first set in motion by self-intuition. First comes the primal act [*der Urakt*], or the ego as the infinitely producing activity, i.e., the "epitome of all reality" [*Inbegriff aller Realität*] (380-81). The absolute ego, however, seeks to posit itself as self-consciousness, that is, "for itself." For Schelling, the meaning of self-intuition implies that self-intuition is the power that can limit the primal act's infinite producing and posit it "for itself," but "the ego as ego is only limited by the fact" (402-9) that "it intuits itself as such, for an ego is only what it is for itself" (382–83). More precisely, this occurs through self-intuition's positing of a negation into the infinite activity, through the positing of a "boundary" [*Schranke*] that "can be expanded into infinity" (383–84), and makes possible the occurrence of "an infinite becoming" [*eines undendlichen Werdens*] (ibid.).[6] For, the limit brings about a "duplicity" (392–93), the duplicity of the "real" activity that, although limited by a boundary, in itself proceeds to infinity, and the infinite, "ideal" activity that forever transcends the boundary. The spontaneity of reason constitutes itself on the basis of this productive strife that is initiated by self-intuition and fulfills itself "preconsciously." According to this "tendency" self-intuition necessarily fulfills itself as a system because "the ego is the infinite tendency to intuit itself" (400–401; 404–5; 418–19).

The desire to intuit itself without the intuiting ego initially knowing that it is the object of intuition is the beginning of the genesis of intelligence. The path begins with a first epoch of "feeling intuition" [*empfindende Anschauung*]; it progresses to a second epoch, "productive intuition"; and raises itself to a higher power until, in a third epoch, intelligence frees itself through the act of "absolute abstraction" from its producing so that free reflection, concept, judgement, and schematism are constituted. The pathway then begins anew when through "the activity of intelligence upon itself" (533–34), through the self-determining act of freedom, the now consciously intuiting ego intuits itself as actively producing. This ego acts according to concepts since it is now practical consciousness; it changes the world that had already shown itself to be the product of intuiting "in a transcendental past" (408–9).

Reason's will to realize itself through practical intuition finds its expression with regard to the composition of the system in the fact that self-intuition gradually brings forth higher powers within itself, in that it increasingly becomes "for itself," that is, objective. In this process the transcendental philosopher is repeatedly presented with a new "task" in which he has to supply a "transcendental explanation" for such questions as, "how does the ego come to intuit itself as limited," or "how does the ego come to intuit itself as productive." The tendency on the part of intelligence to intuit itself can come to rest only in a complete self-intuition, and this is the aesthetic intuition of the genius, as I shall show later. In the meaning of self-intuition lies the necessity that it be developed into this perfect form.

Another connotation of "self-intuition," along with that of a power that limits "all reality," was tied to self-intuition for Schelling. This connotation was that self-intuition is able to "set bounds for itself" [*sich einschränken*] out of freedom, which means out of its own necessity. It is the power of self-intuition that legitimates the concept and composition of the system for all the successive stages up to the stage of individuality (cf. 551–52). Because reason emerges as a self-restricting self-intuition in the construction of its own lawfulness, all of its concepts are "kinds of intuitions" (513–14) and as such they are, in Schelling's words, mere "restrictions [*Einschränkungen*] of intellectual intuition" (370–71). Furthermore, empirical consciousness can only be conceived of as a restriction, a limitation of pure self-consciousness (374–75), just as the world and the things in the world are "only modifications of the ego's activity that is restricted in various ways" (375–76). The meaning of self-intuition includes this necessity of the totality's increasing restriction of itself and thus of its further evolution. The thesis that its evolution necessarily leads to a system follows from the basic supposition that in the pure act of self-consciousness as an "absolute synthesis" all of its ways of acting are comprehended in their lawfulness from the very beginning. In this form of "concrete totality" (388) they are gathered together in the modes of the ego "in itself," and that precisely as such, they have the urge to become "for itself" with regard to the ego through intuition.

These are a few aspects that for Schelling are contained in the meaning of this fundamental concept. They show that the absolute principle of "self-intuition" necessarily evolves as a system, a consequence that Hegel would have denied. In discussing the "method" of the *System of Transcendental Idealism* in the second section of this investigation, I shall illustrate how it is necessary in Schelling's view for self-intuition to develop into a system.

At this point, though, the following question poses itself: If one supposes that the necessity for the development into a system is contained in this principle, how is philosophy able to reconstruct this principle, if it is, as Schelling emphasized, something essentially "nonobjective," something that, as he expressly stated, is "not *reflected* through anything" (350–51) and "never attains consciousness" (600–601), but rather is something that is only the object of an "eternal presupposition in acting" (600–601)? Here I must confine myself to the remark that the transcendental philosopher discovers intellectual intuition to be his principle, and that consequently it must "continually accompany" (369–70) his philosophizing. Intellectual intuition is the "substrate" for his philosophizing and the "organ for transcendental thought," which aims at "making that which is not otherwise an object into an object through freedom" (ibid.). The transcendental philosopher must then allow this spontaneity, this original process of constitution—the "action of intelligence according to determinate laws" (350–51)—to come to be through his own production. Schelling prescribed that the philosopher's "imitative constructing" [*nachahmendes Konstruieren*] (397–98) always has to be a reflection "in intellectual intuition" (351–52). What kind of philosophical reflection is this? Why is "the proper sense in which this philosophy must be comprehended the aesthetic one" (350–51)? How is this philosophizing essentially related to art (627–28)? How does it take the latter for its "organon" (ibid.)?[7] Reflecting "in" intellectual intuition does not divide, but rather unites because Schelling determined theoretical reason, the form under which philosophy is fulfilled, as imagination. Imagination in turn projects "ideas" [*Ideen*] "on the behalf of freedom" (558–59), it is determined to be "the only faculty through which we are capable of conceiving of and conjoining contradictions" (625–26). Within the framework of this analysis I cannot further investigate how transcendental philosophy determines itself as essentially "productive" and even "creative" on the basis of this synthesis of intuition, imagination, and reflection. I cannot pursue the question of whether and how this synthesis distinguishes itself from the synthesis of reflection and intuition that Hegel conceived of in the *Differenzschrift* as "transcendental intuition" (I, 178, 194). In order to characterize the conception of the *System of Transcendental Idealism* more closely, I must instead trace a few of the steps that, within this "history of self-consciousness," lead through successively emerging stages of "failure" (III, 536–37) up to the last stage—the fulfillment of the "task of philosophy" in overcoming dichotomy.

In his philosophy of nature, Schelling had previously attempted to overcome the "division" of nature and the forces of consciousness in a fundamental science that begins with the pure subject-object. There he had demonstrated how the objective subject-object is resolved in a dynamic succession that leads to intelligence—first to the form of the laws of nature, and then in the highest power to reflection, to self-conscious reason. There he had presented evidence that that which is objective and unconscious is essentially akin to that which is subjective, to intelligence, in that there is a "correspondence" [*Übereinstimmung*] between them. Schelling thus maintained that he had overcome Fichte's Idealism, which is purported to have been merely subjective.

The second basic science, the Transcendental System, concerns itself with that "nature which is consciously productive" (634). Its task consists in exhibiting for cognition the foundation of the correspondence between the "complete comprehension of everything merely *objective* in our knowledge" (375) and that which is subjective, that is, intelligence. The subject-object must show itself to be not only "the absolute certainty through which all else is mediated" (346–47), not merely a "principle of explanation" (342–43) for all knowledge; it must prove itself to be the "ground of all reality" (ibid.), the "real ground of the harmony between subject and object" (600-601). Following Fichte as it does, this demonstration is and must be an "expansion" (cf. 330–31) on his *Wissenschaftslehre* [*Doctrine of Science*]. This is achieved through the "factual proof" of a deduction from the principle "I am" (377). This demonstration must exhibit not only the conditions for self-consciousness but also a "whole system of knowledge" in the form of a "history of consciousness" (399), and furthermore it must exhibit "how, for example, the objective world with all of its determinations, i.e. history, etc." (378–79) develop themselves from pure self-consciousness without any external influences. For this purpose, the "main objects of knowledge" (330) must be reconstructed according to the "fundamental axioms of Transcendental Idealism" as a succession of actions performed by intelligence, from the lowest to the highest power.

In the "System of Theoretical Philosophy," in which that which produces and intuits does not become the object as such (cf. 534–35), the production takes place "beyond consciousness" (536–37). The structure of the representation of the objective world with all of its determinations is the result of the strife between mental activities [*geistigen Tätigkeiten*], a strife that is carried out in a "transcendental past" (cf. above pp. 39–41). Its parallel is the constitution of matter as well as organisms by means of an increasingly productive intuition. In the "System of Practical Philosophy" the topic is the ego that has already torn itself away from its unconscious production and has elevated itself above all objects (cf. 534–35), an ego that is now taken as practical intelligence determined in its "acting upon itself" (cf. 533–34ff.). In order to constitute itself as an "actual" practical consciousness, the ego deduces, with reference to "absolute willing" (556–57ff.) and its "appearance" (564–65), i.e., transcendental self-determination" (533–34), how such practical consciousness is produced through the influence of other conscious intelligent beings (554–55) that have a concept of willing. Within this constitution, an opposition arises between the consciousness of being in autonomous subjection to the demands of moral law (cf. 573–74) and the consciousness of being determined by the natural drive for happiness [*Glückseligkeit*] (574-75), which is directed toward an external world (581–82) that is independent of consciousness. This is the opposition that transforms "absolute will" into "voluntary choice" [*Willkür*] (575–76). But how can the voluntary choice of a single rational being, this "act of freedom" with which all consciousness begins (ibid.), this "holiest of all things" (581–82), be protected from being destroyed by the voluntary choice of other individuals? This question is the subject of the deduction of the "mutual interaction" [*Wechselwirkung*] (582–83ff.) of the various individuals who as a species attempt to realize "One Ideal" (cf. above p. 3). They attempt to institute a universal legal order for all nations (588–89ff.) and in the realization of "history," they experience the contradiction between freedom and necessity. This contradiction is constituted, on the one hand, by a blind or concealed necessity (586–87, 594–95) in the form of history's lawfulness, and in this necessity Schelling saw an explanation for the unconscious accomplishment of an "absolute synthesis" (see above p. 8) of all arbitrary and selfish actions on the part of the various individuals (598–99). This synthesis represents that which is common to all, that which is "objective." On the other hand, there is freedom, the "free play" of the actions of individuals as well as of nations (586–87). The conflict between necessity and freedom is meant to be solved by postulating an "*absolute identity*" (600–601). Since there is, however, no duplicity in this identity, and since duplicity is the condition for all consciousness, this identity can never attain consciousness. It is the final ground for the "pre-established harmony" that reigns in history, the harmony between freedom, that which determines, and that which is objective (i.e. the necessary lawfulness) (cf. above p. 10). This absolute identity is God who is *above* both of them and reveals himself in three periods of history, but who for the sake of freedom never fully manifests himself (cf. 603–4; also, above p. 35).

According to the "Fundamental Propositions Concerning Teleology," "organic nature" is then transcendentally explained as a product that is unconsciously brought forth through purposes and ends, although the result appears to have been consciously constituted (607ff.). "For" the living being itself, however, there is no appearance of this identity between unconscious and conscious activity, and certainly not for the consciousness of an ego. By contrast, the aesthetically productive intuition, the aesthetic intuition of the genius, is such that "the ego is simultaneously unconscious and conscious *for itself* in one and the same intuition" (611). This is precisely the identity sought by transcendental philosophy. The "Fundamental Propositions Concerning the Philosophy of Art" deduces that aesthetic production simultaneously realizes itself consciously when considered subjectively, and unconsciously when considered objectively: it is conscious as far as the production is concerned, and unconscious in view of its product (613–14). Furthermore, a genius knows that a "dark and unknown force" contributes objectivity to the work of art that he has consciously formed (616–17). This "simultaneity" attains visible form in an art work. Schelling wrote: "Only a work of art can reflect for me that which cannot otherwise be reflected, the absolute identity . . ." (625-26).

In order to understand the whole conception of the Transcendental System, it is important to see that the "original ground of all harmony between subject and object," the absolute principle, is completely removed from the sphere of subjectivity by the work of art and becomes completely objective (628–29). Even more important is the fact that, through the deduction of aesthetic intuition, the presentation as a whole proves itself to be a "system." In the *Differenzschrift* Hegel demanded as one requirement for a system that "that which is constructed in consciousness as absolute must be something conscious and unconscious at the same time" (I, 178), a requirement that presumably also holds for the system as a whole. Schelling's Transcendental System finds its completion in a similar manner. In aesthetic intuition a principle has been deduced that is the supreme activity of self-consciousness (630) because it is, as had been explicitly postulated at the outset, "simultaneously conscious and unconscious activity . . . *in consciousness itself*" (III, 349–50). Furthermore, because it is essentially akin to the philosopher's intellectual intuition (see below p. 46), it corresponds to the point "where we ourselves stood when we began to philosophize" (628–29, 389–90). This completely satisfies Hegel's requirements for a system. It is then all the more noteworthy that Hegel did not even mention the aesthetic activity and its product in the *Differenzschrift*, as well as a number of other aspects in this system, especially its preconscious stages. His brief remarks concerning the relationship between art, religion, and speculation (I, 270) are already guided by motives directed toward a philosophy of identity.

One important outcome for Schelling was that the philosopher's intellectual intuition becomes objective in aesthetic intuition. Although the philosopher's "inner intuition" is essentially "nonobjective," by being raised to the power of aesthetic intuition, it attains a "universal, generally recognized, and undeniably absolute objectivity" (III, 624–25). Thus, it is not only the nonobjective absolute principle on which all transcendental philosophy rests that is "called forth into consciousness" (624–25). As absolute it also becomes the entire mechanism that philosophy has deduced (625–26). Schelling's statements here may be viewed as a "justification" of his transcendental philosophy in contrast to other contemporary forms of philosophy—or as Hegel put it, of his system as a "proper instrument" (I, 178) for overcoming the predominant dichotomies.

Artistic production is capable of completely overcoming the infinite opposition of activities through the finite production of an ideal world of art (III, 626–27). Transcendental philosophy, by presenting the productive intuition that initiates and then overcomes contradiction in the "real world," performs the same task. Within this "kinship" [*Verwandschaft*] (627–28) art is nevertheless superior to philosophy in that it is capable of externally, objectively presenting that which philosophy can only subjectively attain (627–28, 628–29). Dieter Jähnig, in particular, has concentrated on this relationship between philosophy and art.[8] For our understanding of the entire structure of the transcendental system, however, there is one aspect that is perhaps even more important: In aesthetic intuition, conscious and unconscious activity become objective *in one and the same intuition* (611); and furthermore, in aesthetic intuition the ego becomes "simultaneously conscious and unconscious *for itself*" (ibid.). As Schelling himself remarked, it is here that one finds the solution "to the entire (the supreme) problem of transcendental philosophy (the explanation of the correspondence between subject and object)" (610–11).

We are now able to see the special manner in which Schelling attempted to respond to the "task of philosophy" and to overcome "dichotomy"—and, furthermore, we are able to see the limitations of this attempt. His "Final Remarks on the System" (628–29) bear witness to the fact that he himself did not think that the overcoming of dichotomy in artistic production suffices to overcome the division prevailing in historical and social conditions (see above p. o). Since the system is supposed to have shown that art alone is capable of "objectifying with universal validity" that which philosophy can only present subjectively, it has to be expected that philosophy "must flow back into the universal ocean of poetry" from which it had proceeded. Moreover, the return of philosophy to poetry would supposedly be mediated by mythology, which existed "before the division took place that now appears to be irresolvable" (628–29). But, how a new mythology was supposed to arise, since it can only be the invention of a "new people that represents only one *Author*, as it were," is a "problem," he explained, "whose solution is to be sought only in the future fate of the world and the further course of history" (ibid.).

II

SINCE IT IS my intention to relate Hegel's *Phenomenology* to Schelling's Transcendental System, above all with respect to the latter's method, I would now like to deal with an important aspect of this method, the relationship of the philosophical ego to that ego which is taken as the theme of philosophical presentation, i.e. as philosophy's "object" (629–30). The latter ego is the one Schelling called an "objective ego" in his *Munich Lectures of 1828* (X, 98). These lectures and the *Lectures in Erlangen of 1822* have been decisive determining factors in the interpretation of the Transcendental System until now, especially with regard to this relationship.[9] I am convinced, however, that Schelling depicted his earlier position here in a manner that is not completely faithful to the text of the Transcendental System.

In the *Munich Lectures* the relationship between the "philosophical ego" and the "objective ego" is compared to the one that holds "between the student and the master" in the "Socratic dialogues" (ibid.). This characterization has contributed to the false opinion that the Transcendental System concerns two distinct natural individuals with different experiences.

There is no doubt that in the Transcendental System a distinction is made between the philosophical ego and the ego that it thematizes. This distinction is expressed by the distinction between the term "we," on the one hand, and the ego whose positings are supposed to become "for itself," on the other hand. Schelling also declared that the ego must be "led to the point where it is posited with all the determinations that are contained in the free and conscious act of self-consciousness" (III, 450–51). The investigation must proceed until "the consciousness of our object coincides with our own consciousness" (389–90). Accordingly, transcendental philosophy is said to be "completed" only when "the ego becomes just as much an object for itself as it is for the philosopher" (452–53).

This "allotment of roles and tasks" is in reality, however, merely a "rhetorical figure" for argumentation and serves only to express a point I have already emphasized: that the essence of the ego consists in its becoming objective. In order to illustrate this genesis of self-objectification, a distinction between two "standpoints" in respect to one and the same ego is introduced (402–3). The standpoint of the transcendentally philosophizing ego is the one that performs the reconstruction of reason's original self-constitution by disclosing the conditions for the constitution of self-consciousness. By means of a "free imitation" (396–97) of the original succession in the "first series" of actions, and by means of a reconstruction of them in a "second series," the necessity (357–58) operative within the mechanism of the original genesis is to be demonstrated. Since philosophy's theme is the ego and the ego is nothing other than what it is for itself, however, the philosopher has to halt at each new stage in his reconstruction and inquire to what extent and in what sense that which has been reconstructed has become "for itself" at this stage. In relation to himself, the philosopher places himself in the position of someone else. Because he continually adopts the viewpoint of his object (cf. 402–3), he claims to have accepted the role of an observer, of "looking on" [*Zusehen*] (472–73), although he is the agent of this reconstruction. The important thing is to note that the transcendental philosopher's only concern here is with that which he "freely produces" (cf. 350–51), his "own free constructions" (371–72).

It would be completely false to envisage a "history of cultivation" [*Bildungsgeschichte*] here on account of the references to the philosophical ego as "guiding" the objective ego, or later to a "Socratic dialogue." If the genesis described here were such a history, this would imply certain consequences that do not hold for the Transcendental System. For instance, after the philosopher has discovered that the idea of an immutably presented world, which is accompanied by a feeling of compulsion, is only the result of a strife between various mental [*geistige*] activities, consciousness would have to see through the illusion of this idea. The transcendental philosopher's only concern is, however, as Schelling stated, to demonstrate the "inevitability of the delusion" (351–52), that it is a "necessary illusion," and not to overcome false consciousness as a stage that must be surpassed. If it were a history of cultivation, then the self-intuition of practical consciousness as a false consciousness would also have to proceed to a further level of consciousness that finds its fulfillment in aesthetic consciousness. In the *Munich Lectures* it is therefore misleading when Schelling declared that philosophy in the Transcendental System was a recollecting, an *anamnesis*, for the objective ego, or when Schelling's interpreters spoke, as many have done so, of consciousness's "labor of coming to itself" (X, 93).

Finally, we have to clarify the source of the "law for the continuing process of determination" according to this method. In the *Transcendental System of Idealism*, as well as in the *Munich Lectures*, Schelling explained this continuing determination on the basis of a contradiction immanent within the ego, namely the contradiction that it is simultaneously finite and infinite, limited and unlimited. We have already pointed out that, in order to become "for itself," to become an ego, the original infinite activity must intuit itself; it must posit itself as a subject. In positing itself as a subject, it makes itself into an object, into something finite and bounded, into something other than what it is. For Schelling's later reflection, the ego's inability to ever "gain possession" of itself as a subject is the "fundamental contradiction" [*der Grundwiderspruch*], "the misfortune of all being," "the primal contingency," the "dissonance" (X, 101). This "never being able to gain control of itself," however, represents a "movement that continues to proceed and move on." The subject-object is that which is desired in this movement from the outset, and, Schelling added in response to Hegel's famous polemic in the preface to the *Phenomenology*, this desire is the starting point for the whole process, "the pistol from which it is shot" (149).

What did Schelling see as the "law of progress" for the method of the Transcendental System, as well as for the method of the *Philosophy of Nature*? The subject "A" that must posit itself as "A" in "B" in order to become objective does not remain a simple "A." According to Schelling, it becomes something "*superior to itself*" (103). He adds the following remark to this assertion: "That which is superior is always and necessarily the comprehension and recognition of that which is subordinate. . . ."

In the Transcendental System the strife between the contrary activities is resolved by a third, mediating activity for the sake of the monad's unity, an activity "*which is suspended between opposing directions*" (III, 392). The self-conscious ego continually reasserts itself anew. We may suppose—although Schelling did not clearly state it—that this results from the activity of "imagination" (cf. 557–58, 625–26). By contrast, when a "comprehending and recognizing" [*Begreifen und Erkennen*] of that which is subordinate is spoken of in the *Munich Lectures*, one should note that this does not refer to a comprehending and recognizing on the part of the philosophical subject, but rather to a law that "resides in the absolute subject" (X, 108). In fact, the possibility is expressly excluded that the philosopher is referred to here (ibid.). Does this then mean that now the law of continuing progress in determination can only be explained for Schelling by means of a movement that, because it is referred back to the preceding stages, has to determine them in their opposition in order to mediate them? Does this mean that this movement has the structure of a negative self-reference such as that which underlies reflection and concept in Hegel's thought?

I have attempted to illustrate the conception of Schelling's transcendental philosophy by exploring the meaning of its basic notion, self-intuition. As a result of this inquiry the question arises whether—at least in line with Schelling's later views—reason that constructs itself as self-intuition requires a structure that is alien to intuition for its progress and thus for its systematic completion? This is a question that we must take into account if we are going to try to answer the broader question "How is a systematic philosophy possible?" in the historical form in which it was posed in Schelling's Transcendental System.

III

I BEGAN with the observation that at the time Hegel composed the *Phenomenology* he still shared Schelling's conviction that the "task of philosophy" is to overcome [*aufheben*] the dichotomy between absolute subjectivity and absolute objectivity. Of course, in 1807 Hegel had a completely different view of the possibility for a systematic solution to this task than he did in 1801.[10] In the meantime he had come to the conclusion that the absolute principle, the subject-object, is only truly related to the whole realm of knowledge and conscious action if it does not remain an immobile, immediate Spinozistic substance (cf. *PhG* 19, 9–*10*). It cannot "remain stationary in its beginnings," as Schelling's "idea" does, which "for itself is certainly true" (*PdG* 18, *8*). The subject-object must rather be presented as the "result together with its becoming" (11, *2*) if "that which is true" [*das Wahre*] is to be conceived of and expressed "equally as subject." In Schelling's system, we have seen (see above p. 39), that bounds or negation are posited in the originally absolute and immediate identity. Hegel also conceived of a negativity immanent within the absolute, but thought of it as a relationship between "the one and its other," as a movement of "becoming other than itself together with itself" that relates itself to its negation and to itself (20, *10*). He conceived of the "concept" [*Begriff*] that is realized in a process of self-mediation of the "idea" [*Idee*], and of the subject-object unity as just that "subject" that is realized in and for itself in the philosopher's presentation. For this reason, the question that we posed regarding Schelling's Transcendental System—the question of whether and how its fundamental principle implies the necessity that it be developed into a system—would be completely superfluous here. The "concept," the "subject," *is* as developed self-mediation: the scientific system *is* "the true form in which there is truth" (12, *3*). Regarding the philosopher, it must be noted that for Schelling, absolute identity is disclosed only in intellectual intuition, and is thus manifested only to those rare few—those "born under a lucky star" [*die Sonntagskinder*], as Hegel mockingly remarked[11]—who have a faculty that is akin in its essence to aesthetic intuition. For Hegel, however, reflection is the form of natural consciousness. Of course, this natural reflection must be transformed from a reflection based on understanding into an "absolute" reflection because only the latter is capable of presenting the concept as concept. In the *Differenzschrift*, the stages toward the transformation to the suitable "instrument of philosophizing" demanded there are merely counted off, so to speak; the *Phenomenology*'s great achievement is that it is able to present the succession of stages of experience, which are required by the concept, in such a way that the result, "absolute reflection," is "scientifically necessary."

Schelling's *System of Transcendental Idealism* and Hegel's *Phe-*

nomenology of Spirit are usually viewed as parallel works. The following consideration would seem to preclude such a parallel, however: In contrast to the object of Schelling's system, the *Phenomenology*'s object is the becoming, the genesis of absolute knowledge. The *Phenomenology* is not yet the presentation of speculative philosophy and consequently does not claim to fulfill the task of fully overcoming dichotomy, as Schelling's system does. Nevertheless, a comparison of both systems allows important fundamental traits to be seen. I have just pointed out that Hegel's fundamental conception was exoteric (cf. *PhG* 16, *7–8*), in contrast to the more esoteric view that Schelling held. If Schelling's declared standpoint was that of prereflective intuition, then Hegel's standpoint was just as decidedly that of a reflection, which as understanding, analyzes terms in their relationship to one another, and as reason, is a self-relation that negates these related terms and mediates them with each other. Since reflection is the element that understanding shares with absolute knowledge, it is a matter of giving this element its "completion and transparency exclusively through the movement of its becoming" (23, *14*). The fact that this element is such a common ground makes it possible to "justify" the scientific standpoint against a contemporary culture of reflection by means of a scientific presentation. This stage of reflection is therefore said to be able to make use of the "ladder" that science extends to it (25, *14–15*) and to transform itself into absolute knowledge. The fact that intellectual intuition, however, which is carried out only internally, finds a generally recognized objectivity in aesthetic production must suffice as the "justification" for Schelling's Transcendental System.

The difference in the tasks of the two works cannot preclude a comparison of their methods, since the *Phenomenology* is also the presentation of a "genesis," a genesis of even the same principle, the subject-object identity. It can be shown that the "idea" of the entire work is contained in just this principle.[12] What kind of genesis is the *Phenomenology*? In the *Munich Lectures*, Schelling insisted that his Transcendental System was the first to have had a "tendency toward the historical" (X, 93). I have shown, however, that the Transcendental System is history only as the genesis of the transcendentally reconstructed lawfulness found in reason's original self-construction. The *Phenomenology* is by contrast a real history, even if only "under the aspect of the conceptual comprehension of its organization" (*PhG* 564,

493). More precisely, it is a "history of the experience" that consciousness has with itself and, at the same time, a history of spirit in its self-
alienation and subsequent return to itself. It does not deduce a series of
ways in which reason acts, but instead represents a succession of historical forms that, guided by the categories that follow one another, experience the claim to truth inherent in each of these forms. The succession
does not end in a self-intuition in which conscious and unconscious
activity are simultaneously present for consciousness, i.e. in aesthetic
activity and its product, the work of art. Instead, it terminates in the
"form of spirit that knows itself as spirit." This genesis does not construct a preconscious occurrence within a "transcendental past" that
makes real consciousness possible; it begins rather with real consciousness, even if only in its immediate form, sense certainty. As the first
form of consciousness, sense certainty is above all determined by "inorganic nature," and precisely not by an absolute identity that the philosopher has purified from all alien determinations, as is the case with
Schelling's intellectual intuition. In the *Phenomenology* this "purifica-
tion" occurs only gradually in the history of experience and finds its
completion in that form from which everything factual has been removed. The Transcendental System, by contrast, finds its completion
in the fact that there is art.

All these differences can be explained by Hegel's basic conviction
that the absolute principle is the concept in its attainment of total manifestation, and not prereflective self-intuition. Although the uniqueness
of Hegel's concept lies in its having overcome the immobility of Kant's
conception, it is the identity between identity and difference contained
in transcendental apperception that is the principle that Hegel made
dynamic through historical experience and that he presented as modes
of spirit in its self-mediation and in its process of becoming transparent
to itself. In any case, the absolute principle does not emerge as a fundamental proposition or "principle" [*Grundsatz*] that must be posited as
the totality of knowledge in the way we have shown necessary in the
Transcendental System. Rather, the absolute principle, "the concept,"
is presented in its operation as a process of self-mediation. In the *Phenomenology*, the concept appears in modes of consciousness, of "appear-
ing" or "phenomenal" knowledge [*erscheinendes Wissens*]. Phenomenal
knowledge then further determines itself in a history of experience until
it reaches that shape in which it comes to know itself as "subject-object,"

until it is absolute knowledge or "conscious identity." This is natural consciousness in the form of knowing, which, in contrast to natural consciousness itself, is subject to a philosophically guided, systematic self-examination and becomes involved in a regular movement according to law. And it is this movement that brings about this progression toward absolute knowledge. Furthermore, this movement guarantees the completeness of the forms that are presented. "Phenomenal knowledge" is the philosopher's theme, his object, and even though the philosopher is here distinguished from phenomenal knowledge in the same terms in which this is done in Schelling's system, through "we" and "for us" as opposed to "for itself," one cannot emphasize strongly enough that "phenomenal knowledge" is capable of having experiences with itself; whereas Schelling's "objective ego" is, as we have shown, nothing other than a "rhetorical figure" that is employed by the philosopher himself. The "objective ego" in the Transcendental System cannot take on an independent role; "phenomenal knowledge," by contrast, is entrusted with the important role of consciously liberating itself from its "inorganic nature" by means of the "desperation" [*Verzweifelung*] produced by a "self-fulfilling skepticism" (cf. above p. 26). The obtive ego, however, does not discern its "transcendental past," nor can the various powers of its self-intuition lead to the consciousness of absolute identity between subject and object that is postulated by the philosopher.

The "law of continuing progress in determination" [*Gesetz der Fortbestimmung*] in the *Phenomenology* thus rests primarily on the activity of "phenomenal knowledge." The unique structure of this law should be briefly explored by contrasting it with the motive for continuing determination in the Transcendental System.

Here again it is decisive that for Hegel, consciousness has a conceptual nature. "Consciousness for itself, however, is the *concept*" (69, *51*). The objective ego in the Transcendental System can be judged only against the "standard" of the identity between the conscious and unconscious activity in consciousness, according to a standard that the philosopher imposes "from the outside," so to speak. By contrast, due to its conceptual nature, consciousness in the *Phenomenology* is nothing other than its own comparison with itself (cf. 72, *53–54*). In the execution of its "self-examination," the form and content of knowledge are measured against the "objectivity" that is inherent as a standard in the structure of consciousness itself. "Consciousness provides its standard in itself" (71, 53). This standard changes when consciousness corrects its knowledge: That which was "in itself" [*an sich*] at first, is now demoted to "being in-itself for-itself" [*für es an sich Sein*]. This change in the standard, this transition to a new standard is "experience." The necessary connection between the new standard and the previous one remains concealed, since the consciousness that has the experience thinks that it has cast the "old" one into the "empty abyss." It is precisely this experience that is the realization of the "law of further determination"; phenomenal knowledge's inability to discern this law, which lies inherent within it, is another matter. In any case, whereas the "objective ego" thematized by the philosopher in the Transcendental System has no function at all in this further determination, in the *Phenomenology* it is the experience of phenomenal knowledge as "comprehended in experience" that stimulates the process of further determination.

But surely the presentation of the necessity of further determination would not be possible if it were not discerned by the philosopher. His "contribution" [*Zutat*] consists in "viewing the issue" [*die Betrachtung der Sache*] (74, 55–56), because he does not hold the result of each particular examination—the noncorrespondence between knowledge and that which is "in itself," i.e. the untenability of the standard—to be an empty nothingness as "phenomenal consciousness" does. He sees it rather as the "*nothingness of that from which it results*" (ibid.). The philosopher recognizes that the experience of the nothingness of the previous object, of the first "in itself," contains as its result the new object. He recognizes that phenomenal knowledge's experience of the noncorrespondence between the previously dominant spheres of objectivity, or truth, and its knowledge of this objectivity is an antithetic movement. He recognizes that the "new object" is nothing other than the synthesis that results from the antithetic movement of experience. This dialectic of "*determinate* negation" (69, 51), which is the foundation for phenomenal knowledge's experience, contains the "law of a continuing progress in determination," which has been the object of our inquiry. For this law not only governs the genesis of a single particular shape but guides "the whole series of shapes of consciousness in their necessity" (74, 56). For the later Schelling, the Transcendental System's law of further determination consisted in the fact that "the absolute subject" reasserts itself anew in each objective form by "recognizing and conceiving" it as "superior" to the previous one. When we noted that accepting this view implies that there must also be some sort of "knowledge" in the realm of preconsciousness that has a structure of self-relation, i.e. of the concept, this did not by any means imply that the concept plays the same role according to the method of the Transcendental System that it does in the *Phenomenology*. In the Transcendental System, it does not serve as a "standard" that consciousness gives to itself. It is also important that this be emphasized because the "law of continuing progress in determination" in the *Phenomenology* depends on the *Logic* in developing its categories, its "essences," or "moments." This logical development can be recognized by the philosopher, and it is his task to actively further this development. This can be documented not only by passages in the preface, but also by the section at the end of the *Phenomenology* (566, 488) where Hegel spoke of an additional "contribution" that the philosopher makes.[13] In this section, a "gathering" [*Versammlung*] of the various moments and an "adherence [*Festhalten*] to the concept in the form of concept" is demanded of the philosopher. The philosopher is supposed to retain the categorical determinations or essences, the "moments," such as "being-in-itself," "being-for-itself," "self-sameness;" in short, he is supposed to gather and retain them as the process of self-mediation, as the very process of the concept in its self-determination. This means that in the *Phenomenology* the absolute principle, according to the law "inherent within it," securely and decisively guarantees that the movement described above necessarily leads to the goal of the system. The system in the *Phenomenology*, just like the one in Schelling's "Transcendental Idealism," is based on the supposition that there is a principle within empirical consciousness—namely, the spontaneity of self-constructing reason, the movement of an identity that is differentiated within itself—which develops itself into a system. Already in the *Phenomenology*, Hegel asserted the possibility of systematic philosophy, just as Schelling had done in the *System of Transcendental Idealism*.

In closing, I might add the following remark: Schelling's so-called "Aesthetic Idealism" has been viewed to be "speculatively unsatisfactory" by Kroner,[14] and as a "solution for lack of any other" [*Verlegenheitslösung*] by Schulz,[15] not primarily because there is no reference to art in Schelling's development after 1809, but rather because the philosophy of art is said to "have veiled the questions concerning the knowability of absolute knowledge."[16] These interpretations measure Schelling's basic notions according to the standard of Hegel's basic notion, that of "the concept," of absolute reflection. It is in the concept that subjectivity indeed realizes itself through the self-mediation of its content, and, in its knowing, the principle provides its own foundation. In the Transcendental System, however, self-intuition has no such *telos*. There is rather a preconscious operation that belongs to reason as self-intuition, and the highest power of this operation is characterized by the idea of "genius." This is the phenomenon that Schelling called "pure contingency" in the final lines of his System (III, 633–34). Here we see a further implication contained in his basic thought: the aspiration toward a sort of "knowledge" that *cannot* be grasped by thought.

I shall not here pursue Schelling's further development in this direction. The purpose of this section was to show that, at the outset of German Idealism, Schelling employed the basic notion of intuition to conceive of something radically different from Hegel's basic notion of reflection and of the concept. Both philosophers' ideas were held to be principles of reason, and the realization of each of their basic conceptions by the philosopher was intended as a response to the type of task required of philosophy, and to the "need of philosophy" [*Bedürfnis der Philosophie*] to overcome the dichotomy prevalent at the time. There are certain contemporary movements in philosophy that, in attempting to counteract the dichotomy predominant today, almost without any reservations exclusively orient themselves toward Hegelian reflection and "the concept."[17] Perhaps, however, "practical philosophy" today would do well to recall the significance of the notion that underlies Schelling's Transcendental System—the notion of self-intuition.

3

The Task of Schelling's
Philosophical Inquiries into the
Essence of Human Freedom

I

IN HIS WORK *The Difference between Fichte's and Schelling's Systems of Philosophy*,[1] Hegel stated that the task, "the need of philosophy," consisted in overcoming [*Aufhebung*][2] the dichotomy that the philosophy of reflection had brought forth in his day. In the "development of culture" [*Bildung*] in the modern age, this philosophy had "rigidified" the traditional oppositions, especially the opposition between "intelligence and nature." He stated that Schelling had already responded to this task by constructing the "objective subject-object" in his philosophy of nature and the "subjective subject-object" in his transcendental philosophy as the two sides of his system as a whole (cf. I, 178, 205ff.). The younger Schelling had indeed previously demonstrated that nature is not a *res extensa* in the Cartesian sense, that it is not a mathematical realm bereft of spirit and separated from the *res cogitans*, the mind or spirit, by an unbridgeable gap.[3] Nature is rather a spirit that, in a dynamic series of stages from inorganic matter up to consciousness, is similar to an ego. It is thus altogether a will, and, as such, it is "freedom," even if in a "suspended" [*aufgehoben*] mode (cf. III, 376). To put it another way: reality in nature is from the very outset ideality. For Schelling "nature" was the *natura naturans* that itself produces its *naturata*. It was life in its living genesis. By demonstrating this, he had attempted to found an "Objective Idealism" in opposition to Fichte's "Subjective Idealism." In retrospect, he remarked in the *Inquiries* (VII,

351) that one must not only demonstrate "that activity, life, and freedom alone are the only things that truly exist . . . , it is rather necessary
to prove the opposite, that everything that exists (Nature, the world of
things) is based on activity, life, and freedom, or—to use Fichte's expression—not only that the ego is everything, but that, to the contrary,
everything is also ego." In this context, Schelling attained an insight
that is decisive for the thesis of this essay, the insight that "to make
thought, freedom, the sum and substance of philosophy" would be to
give science a "more powerful impulse in a new direction than any previous revolution" (ibid.). Regarding his own motivation, he declared:
"Only he who has tasted freedom can feel the desire to make everything
analogous to it, to propagate it throughout the whole universe" (ibid.).

The Transcendental System, which by means of an "intellectual intuition" reconstructs the genesis of the ego in its self-construction,
shows how, within the dimension of theoretical philosophy, "spirit" or
"mind" [*Geist*] presupposes nature. More importantly, within the dimension of practical philosophy it then shows how, contrariwise, mind
has the power to elevate [*aufheben*] that which is merely natural to a
"second nature." In the deduction of history, i.e. of the action of the species (see above p. 3), freedom emerges in its realization as that which
unites nature, the realm of necessity, with spirit or mind. The central
motif among the various interrelated motifs in the Transcendental System is the following: "Everyone who has attentively followed us this far
can see for himself that the beginning and the end of this philosophy is
freedom, that which is absolutely indemonstrable and is proved only
through itself" (III, 376).

Had Schelling not then already responded to the "need of philosophy" as defined by Hegel? Had he not found the connection, the system
(see above p. 34), by showing the predominance of freedom to be identical in both realms and by then showing it to be the foundation for
their unity? Was this not the system that had been repeatedly sought
after in various conceptions ever since Parmenides set out to inquire
into the relationship between Being and thought?

Since Plato, however, metaphysics has not been content with the
demonstration that the relationship between nature and the human
spirit, or Being[4] and thought, is one of identity, a special sort of unity. It
has been demanded that this unity be in turn founded in a being that
is supreme and itself has no other foundation. The determination of

beings as such—ontology—must be founded in theology.[5] In Neo-Platonism the conviction arose that the conjunction between Being and thought, nature and mind, this "system," must find its final foundation in something that is absolved from finitude and reigns over both of these realms. Schelling also stood in this tradition. In the deduction of the concept of history in the Transcendental System, he had accordingly already directed his view to an "absolute identity" that is infinite and beyond history; his view was directed to that which "can never attain consciousness" for mere knowledge, i.e. to God (600, cf. 368, 379). The fact that there are works of art (see above pp. 45ff.) concludes this system because these alone reflect the "absolute identity" in a universally accessible manner. In his further development, which was influenced by Spinoza's system, Schelling became convinced that he could not be satisfied with a demonstration of the identity between nature and mind through the concept of freedom. He became convinced that it was not sufficient to direct one's view from the finite human mind and created nature toward absolute identity. He came to the insight that one must start with the absolute—God—who for Spinoza is the unity of Being (the Cartesian *res extensa*), the real, and mind (the Cartesian *res cogitans*), the ideal. By proceeding from the essence of divine Being, one must show that the condition of the possibility of finite nature and of the finite mind unites *both* of them in itself. It must be proven that, because of the unity of mind and Being in God, everything is at once real and ideal. A genuine proof of identity within the finite realm is only possible if this unity can be shown to be a manifestation of divine identity.[6]

In view of Spinoza's system, Schelling recognized quite clearly that the proof of freedom's predominance in both realms, in nature and in spirit, can be convincing only if the appearances of finite freedom are founded in divine freedom. Therefore, Spinoza's *causa sui*, the freedom of the absolute as absolute "groundlessness," must previously have been conceived of as such if freedom within the finite realm is to be secured. In the *Presentation of My System* (1802), in the *Further Presentation*, in the *Lectures Concerning the Methods of Academic Studies* (1803), in the *Presentation of the Philosophy of Art* (1802), and in the dialogue *Bruno* (1802), Schelling had taken great pains to model himself after Spinoza (IV, 113) and to conceive the absolute, God, as the unity of mind and nature, as the unity between the ideal and the real. From the standpoint

of absolute reason, it is obvious that both of these aspects are "not actual" [*unwirklich*] in God's essence, and that their relationship with regard to each other is one of "absolute indifference,"[7] or "absolute disin-
terest." At the same time, divine Being is the "universe," "absolute
totality" (125, 129), and contains nature and the finite intellect as
forces within itself. All finite and singular beings, the plurality, are thus
simultaneously real and ideal within this unity of a qualitative identity.
This does not mean that there cannot be quantitative differences with
regard to such particular dimensions as, for instance, the dimension of
inorganic beings, that of organic beings, or that of consciousness and
mind. Both realms—nature and the world of human spirit—are akin to
each other according to their eternal idea. They are thus bound in a
systematic relationship to one another and their oppositions are resolved in the absolute identity of divine Being.

Why did Schelling come to proceed beyond this "System of Identity?" In particular, we must ask how it happened that, in the dialogue
Bruno (1802) for instance, the idea of a "disjunction" [*Absonderung*] of
finitude was transformed so that there the "Fall" appears as a "stage"
(VI, 471) in which finite freedom finds a factual form. Why did this lead
to the approaches that abandoned the Philosophy of Identity (V, 429)
such as those proposed in the treatise *Philosophy and Religion* (1804)?
And how did these lead in turn to the *Aphorisms*, which introduced the
Philosophy of Nature (1805–1806),[8] to the first version of *The Ages of
the World* (1806), and, above all, to the ideas proposed in the work *Philosophical Inquiries Concerning the Essence of Human Freedom* (1809)?
As far as an account of the various influences involved in various stages
in Schelling's thought are concerned, the answer appears to be simple.
Schelling began to read the works of the theosophist Friedrich
Christoph Oetinger as early as 1803. Oetinger, in turn, was familiar
with the writings of the Church Fathers, the mystics, and the cabbala;
with Paracelsus, Emanuel Swedenborg, and the Swabian theologian
Johann Albrecht Bengel; and, above all, with the theosophic mysticism
of Jakob Böhme. During Schelling's stay in Munich from 1805 until
1806, he became acquainted with Böhme's teachings in particular, as
well as with those of St. Martin, Johannes Tauler, Meister Eckhart,
and Nicolaus Cues through Franz von Baader.[9] The irrational, that
which cannot be accounted for, that which is essentially alien and un-
familiar in Being, the demonic and the magical that are to be found in

reality, the undisclosed, uncanny forces slumbering in everything that is forceful and vital, that which is demonically threatening, and in particular, all the terrifying power and reality of evil—all these issues were now taken up as problems, problems presented in the special sort of Christian thought in which Böhme, Oetinger, and Baader related the powers of darkness to the powers of light in the form of Jesus' love. Various questions forced themselves on Schelling: How can one conceive of the Christian God of Creation if his creation is permeated by the powers of darkness? How can the struggle between the powers of darkness and the powers of light be compatible with revelation as it is conceived of in Christianity? Looking back on the System of the Philosophy of Nature, of Transcendental Philosophy, and of the Philosophy of Identity, he was now faced with the question of whether his view of nature and the finite spirit, as well as of the essence of the absolute, had not been completely wrong. If evil is real, and if man can choose evil precisely because he is free, then how can one conceive of a theodicy? How can a system of pantheism be conceived in which God's absolute freedom and infinite goodness are consistent with a human freedom that is finite and capable of evil?[10] Our inquiry is directed toward the "task" of the *Inquiries*. Precisely because of the young Schelling's basic insight that the bond that unites nature and man is freedom, and because his later Philosophy of Identity led him to the conclusion that this freedom must be founded in God's absolute freedom in order to guarantee its systematic cohesion, Schelling's experience of the powers of darkness and the reality of evil now forced on him the task of considering "the essence of human freedom." The task that he faced was also complicated by a further problem. Since, as we have seen, he had learned from Spinoza that the essence of finite beings must be founded in something infinite, an absolute, a "deduction" of human freedom as a faculty for evil could not be achieved in the manner that Schelling had thought possible until then. This means that the primary task of the *Inquiries* lay in a rethinking of the *causa sui* that had been seen as the determination of the absolute, as absolute freedom, such that, in congruence with the theosophic view, one could consequently conceive of a completely different sort of freedom in the finite spirit and in nature.

Schelling was confronted with a much more difficult task than his theosophic predecessors, whose task was not to solve the problem of freedom. Böhme and Oetinger had not experienced the French Revolution, which along with Kant's philosophy had been the decisive event of the age for the students at the Tübingen Seminary. Confronted with the problem of freedom, Schelling had to reintroduce the question of how the absolute is capable of providing a foundation for the finite spirit and for nature in a manner consistent with the historical development that the concept of freedom had undergone. This development had its true beginnings in Kant and in German Idealism. "Until the discovery of Idealism [in which Schelling included Kant] the genuine concept of freedom was lacking in all recent systems, in Leibniz's just as in Spinoza's" (VII, 345, 348). Furthermore, according to Schelling, Idealism is said to have previously developed only "the most general, and, at the same time, the merely formal concept of freedom" (352). For, anyone seeking the content of freedom is left "helpless" by "the doctrine of freedom" proffered there (351, 156).

The first task in the *Inquiries* is thus prescribed to be the determination of the absolute's essence as it is experienced from the theosophic perspective. This is to be accomplished by developing a new concept of freedom, a concept not of human freedom but rather of the freedom of the absolute.

There are serious problems involved in this definition of the task of *Inquiries*. According to its title, the treatise consists of *Philosophical Inquiries into the Essence of Human Freedom*, and precisely not into divine freedom. The very first sentence indicates that the matter of concern is that "most vivid feeling" (399, cf. 336), which is stimulated by the "fact of freedom," and it is expressly stated that the concept of human freedom is "one of the system's dominant focal points" (ibid.). Other passages (340) are even more explicit: The issue is the rescuing of man's freedom[11] and the demonstration of "the specific difference, the determinacy of human freedom" (352).[12] In the elaboration of the system, the only issue is said to be the question of the extent to which the concept of human freedom can be reconciled with divine understanding (337). Completely in line with this determination of the task of the *Inquiries*, contemporary interpreters have emphasized the essence of freedom insofar as it is human; thus Habermas's[13] interest is directed toward the "anthropology" contained in the *Inquiries* and toward the determination of freedom as something human and historical (cf. above pp. 18–32). By contrast, others have focused on Schelling's theosophic predecessors and raised the question concerning the essence of God.

They have failed to note, however, that the determination of the divine essence is a new step for Schelling in the development of the philosophical concept of freedom. It is supposed to perform the function of unifying, justifying, and guaranteeing all finite human freedom, as well as the freedom of nature, by "grounding" them in something infinite and absolute without abolishing the independence of finitude. This novel sense of "grounding" will be developed below.

In my opinion, this new step in the *Inquiries*[14] must be seen in general as a significant step forward. In spite of the importance that the determination of human freedom has from a theosophic perspective, its true significance consists precisely in the fact that it is not constructed in isolation or conceived of only in relation to freedom in nature, but rather that divine freedom provides a basis that is the principle of generation and explanation for everything else. This fits in with Schelling's declaration in the *Stuttgart Private Lectures*: "There is no other principle of explanation for the world than divine freedom" (429, 423).[15]

II

TWO YEARS after the *Inquiries* appeared, Hegel claimed to have fulfilled the above-mentioned desideratum by presenting the *Science of Logic*. In the introduction to this work he wrote, "The *Logic* must therefore be understood as the system of pure reason, as the realm of pure thought. *This realm is the truth unveiled and in and for itself.* For this reason, one can say that its content is the *presentation of God as he is in his eternal essence prior to the creation of nature and the finite spirit*" (III, 1, 35f. 50). This presentation had become possible for him because philosophical thought had progressed along the long pathway of the *Phenomenology* to its "final shape": conceptual, absolute knowing (*PhG*, 556, 485), which therefore had been able to realize the concept as concept.[16] Schelling, by contrast, was of the opinion that such a pathway was not necessary in order to discern by means of an "objective investigation, by means of the development of the primal essence itself, what God is," or as Schelling also says—in order to determine what he is "on his own account" (VIII, 168). For Schelling, God is "what he wills to be" (ibid.). It is solely on the basis of this fact that he concluded that the philosopher's first task consists in "examining his will." The question, "what God wills" is equivalent to the question "what does he want *on his own account* and not on ours" (ibid.).

Such an inquiry into God's will entails an inquiry into the specific character of divine "freedom," i.e. God's freedom "prior to the creation of nature and a finite spirit." Accordingly, the first question is how "God makes himself" (VII, 432)? One must inquire into the occurrence within God prior to the world, into a theogony that is, of course, essentially related to cosmogony (see appendix, p. 83).

This is one of Schelling's central ideas, which is expressed in the *Stuttgart Private Lectures* in the following manner: "And so, to say it in one word: *God makes himself*. And just as certainly as he makes himself, it is certain that he is not something complete and simply present right from the outset; otherwise, he would not need to make himself" (ibid.).

In scholastic terms this would mean that God bears within himself the reason for his existence, but as Schelling observed, "Every philosopher says that" (357). For instance, Spinoza had determined God's absolute substance as *causa sui*. For Spinoza, this *causa* was the one being that exists through its own nature and is determined by nothing other than itself, neither by Being nor by being acted upon. Spinoza's *causa sui* denoted an absolute unboundedness; it was an expression of "freedom from . . . ." In recollection of the tradition, Schelling added the following important remark: "But they speak of this ground as a mere concept without making it into something real and actual" (357f.).

This is precisely what Schelling undertook to achieve in the *Inquiries*. We have seen the significance of this effort to make the "ground" of divine existence into something actual and real (cf. above, p. 61 and note 9), and have traced the influence of the theosophic, magical Christology of Böhme, Oetinger, and Baader. Nevertheless, I am convinced that the meaning that the notion of "life" had for Schelling in particular as well as for the whole age of Romanticism was the decisive factor here, especially in the constitution of the structure of divine freedom.

Schelling conceived of life as a fundamental ontological movement, which is structured within itself, and which in the end is thought of against the background of an *entelechia*-like movement derived from the traditional doctrine of substance or "*ousia*" (see above p. 4). This will be shown more clearly later (p. 80). For now, it is only important to note that for Schelling, just as for the theosophists, life was like a great magician who creates and generates something where before there had been nothing. Life is that which is capable of developing itself on its own and which thus manifests itself by producing luminosity, spirituality, and regularity out of darkness, obscurity, and unruliness. Insofar as it realizes itself by itself, life is *causa sui*. Such self-generation, however, can only occur by means of life's conflict within itself. Wherever there is life, it is a real force that posits something over against itself; it limits itself in order to rediscover itself again as an ideal force out of such opposition and limitation. By doing so, it heals and resolves contradiction. Life is the conflict of oppositions, but at the same time, within this conflict is the immediate unity of the oppositions that shows itself through these oppositions. In the concept of life, Schelling conceived the very same self-movement that was contained for Hegel in negativity; indeed Hegel also often simply termed this movement "life." Schelling used this concept of life to oppose the mechanistic views of his age, which were derived from the historical influence of Cartesianism. This is the reason why we find it over and over again in decisive passages of the *Inquiries*, in the *Stuttgart Private Lectures*, and in the various versions of *The Ages of the World*. In the *Inquiries*, one reads, "But all life has a destiny and is subject to suffering and becoming. . . . Being is aware of itself only in becoming. There is, of course, no becoming in Being . . . but a becoming is necessarily entailed in any realization through opposition" (403). Furthermore, "wherever there is no conflict, there is no life" (400).

Schelling thus determined the essence of God on the basis of this concept of life. "There is a system in divine understanding, but God himself is not a system but a life" (399). Because God is life, he contains an oppositional becoming within himself, an opposition that does not, however, conflict with his unity. Because God does not have an idealistic, logical structure, because he is not "a mere logical abstraction" (394) but rather life, he can only be comprehended as an event, as an inner mobility in which divine Being constitutes itself on its own. Divine Being is not a system in the sense of a totality, as the perfect whole of a dialectical movement of mediation in which thought conceives itself. Instead the absolute must relinquish its completeness, it must be subject to "destiny" (403). As a living God, he is "not only Being" (ibid.) but also "self-becoming." There is one goal here: It is in the interplay of the real and the ideal powers of opposing and healing forces that God constitutes himself atemporally as a person on his own. As a person, he is omnipotent not only in regard to himself, but also in regard to other beings; he attains the power to reveal himself, the power of creation. This step of emerging into Being as a "deed" prior to and beyond all thought (395) is opposed to the seemingly related structure of the Spirit in Hegel's philosophy, which externalizes itself in order to be truly present to itself in its returning to itself.

III

OUR THESIS IS, therefore, that the first step in the *Inquiries* consists in determining the essence of divine freedom, and that this is accomplished within the horizon of the categories of "life."[17] It is thus of great importance to see in general how Schelling proceeded to reach this dimension of freedom. Together with the theosophists, he began with the supposition that, "prior to all grounding and to everything existent," the Godhead is a "nonground" [*Ungrund*] (406). This concept characterizes that state within the process of God's becoming himself in which he is neither Being nor becoming, and thus in no sense a ground, not even for himself. As "nonground," God is the "absence of ground" [*Abgrund*]. In this state, one cannot yet speak of a divine "life," for here God is "prior to all opposition" (ibid.); and without opposition, there is no life. God as the nonground is not even the overcoming of opposition in the sense of an "absolute identity" (ibid.). For this reason, Schelling terms his essence "absolute indifference." Indifference is not in turn a product of opposition, nor does it implicitly contain such oppositions. As the nonground, God is an essence apart from all opposition, an essence "upon which all oppositions shatter" (ibid.).

Does God's being a nonground imply that he is "nothing" in the sense of a *nihil negativum*? Certainly not, for Schelling only spoke of "nonBeing" in regard to oppositions and the ground. What does this concept "nonground" mean? Does it have a function in determining the essence of divine freedom? The determination "nonground" is a "concept of limit" in the true sense of the word; it is a concept that denotes the transitional movement across the threshold that leads from nonBeing into Being. In terms of God, it refers to the transition from God as absolute indifference to God as "eternal oneness" (359). As "eternal oneness" God has left the state of being a "nonground" behind him, the "nonground" is God prior to his self-revelation. The gap that the "transition" from the "nonground" to "eternal oneness" must overcome cannot be bridged by deducing a chain of grounds or reasons. It is a gap that is not accessible to grounds. It rather belongs to the nature of this "transition" that it must be a "leap."[18] Suddenly, like a "bolt of lightning" (VIII, 304), there is "eternal oneness." This oneness is the "seed" (VII, 363) that must be present before any subsequent "development" can take place. I am convinced that God's inexplicable and sudden emergence as eternal oneness is intricately connected with the meaning of his essence, which is, for Schelling, the realization of a special kind of freedom. Indeed it is the lightninglike emergence that characterizes that aspect of freedom which the tradition denotes with the concept of "spontaneity." The emphasis here is not as much on the fact of a "beginning" but rather on a "being able to begin." Why is it possible that there *can be* a beginning at all? This is the deepest mystery in the essence of freedom. Schelling's answer to this question, which still accords the mystery its due, might perhaps be that a beginning can be made because divine freedom emerges in the leap from God as the nonground to God as the "eternal oneness." God's "life," his development, fulfills itself in a dimension that is given its essence through the occurrence of an essentially inexplicable leap, a dimension that, from the outset, is the dimension of absolute freedom. The formation of God's development into a person from his beginnings in absolute oneness can thus only be understood if it is seen to be the formation of divine life as freedom. For this reason, Schelling emphatically asserted that the development of God's "primal Being" is a development of the will. "Willing is primal Being" (350). This determination has indeed been understood as a determination of all finite Being, but this is by no means the case, since Schelling added the remark: "all of the will's predicates apply to it [i.e. the divine essence] alone: inexplicability, eternity, independence from temporality, self-assertion" (ibid.). These are all determinations of the divine essence. The fact that primal Being is will means that divine life is a life based on absolute freedom.[19]

Schelling's presentation of God's absolute self-becoming is couched in anthropomorphic terms. I shall attempt to translate them into an "ontology of life" and interpret this ontology as the construction of the structural framework involved in God's absolute freedom. Various stages must be distinguished here. The first stage concerns the occurrence prior to the eternal deed of self-manifestation (cf. VII, 359). In this stage, God forms himself as a person and—to use transcendental terms—then constitutes within himself the "conditions for the possibility" of revelation, of creation. Within creation itself, one must then distinguish between a "first," "initial" creation (cf. 375, 377) and a "second creation" (cf. 380), which becomes a "lasting" one (378).

Prior to his revelation, God as the "eternal oneness" is, in Schelling's view, the "longing [*Sehnsucht*] to give birth to himself" (353). In revealing himself, God takes a first step by excluding "that which is dark and unconscious from himself" and by "expelling [that which is subordinate in his essence] from himself" (473).[20] Thus, within the divine unity arises an unconscious part of God that is opposed to the consciously "existent" God and that "within God is *not God himself*" (359). A stratum arises that is distinct, although not separable from him. This stratum in God constitutes the "ground of his existence" (358).

For our inquiry into the structure of divine freedom, it is important to note that Schelling took for granted, as it were, that this "first stirring of divine existence" (360), the constitution of the ground for divine existence, must be conceived of as a spontaneously initiated "willing" (cf. above p. 68). Since it has only a presentiment [*ahndet*] of understanding (359), this initial will is compared to "craving and desire" [*Sucht und Begierde*], which are by their very structure an externally oriented striving, and are thus "incapable" of "constituting something lasting on their own" (360). What this "dark ground" wills is to develop itself into light. Since in this respect it is "comparable to the drive of nature in its development" (395), Schelling also called it "nature in God" (358), a term that is meant to refer to that element of necessity in the divine essence on which freedom is founded.

This first step in divine self-creation already has significant implications for our question concerning the essence of divine freedom: namely that it is only through divine omnipotence that the initial will realizes itself in its presentiments. God himself in his existence presupposes this ground for his existence. "But," as Schelling expressly remarked, "on the other hand, God is also . . . prior to the ground, for the ground as such could not be if God did not exist actū" (358). For the construction of the whole framework of absolute freedom, this moment of contradiction is necessary. It is a contradiction that God has posited within his unity by means of the "real principle" that is proper to him—the principle of darkness. The divine essence, however, also originally contains a second, an ideal principle, by means of which light predominates at this stage of the development. Both of these principles are inseparably unified in God. The first stage of the initial creation in this dynamic interaction is the "birth of light" (377) from darkness. This birth must exist as the ground "so that light can be elevated out of it" (ibid.). God is still also present in the ground that has been expelled from him: as the "luminous vision of life" [*leuchtender Lebensblick*] (361) he is present in the will, in the longing of the ground, a longing that has seized this "vision of life" "so that a ground will always remain" (ibid.).

Divine existence is thus realized as light in its dynamic and *entelechia*-like relation to its own ground. It emerges as the luminous form of that representation that shines on and reflects itself, which sees itself in its own "likeness" (360). As "internally reflective (ibid., cf. 396), divine existence has produced itself through a second primal action in God himself. This is the creation of the sphere of objectivity in general, even though the only object possible prior to creation is God himself. "God views himself in his image" (360). He has become objective for himself in self-intuition, as Schelling had indicated already in *Philosophy and Religion* (VI, 40, 42). "Representation" [*Vor-stellung*] is a power that brings about a separation within itself; as such it is the "original understanding" that is the "condition for the possibility" of all creation. As the separation of forces, understanding is active in the ground and awakens the forces that are separate from it, so that it can then expose the unity of the divine vision of life concealed within those forces. This unity is the *idea* of the essence that must be created or "informed" [*eingebildet*] into nature (VII, 362). Divine understanding enlightens the dark principle, it is the "word of that longing" (361). The "eternal spirit" expresses this word, although at this stage of the occurrence of creation in a "merely imperfect manner"; this word is expressed "in nature" (363). It is only in the second power [*Potenz*] of this occurrence, the "realm of history" (377–78), that he completely expressed this word "in mankind" (ibid.). This is the revelation of spirit and thus of God as "actū existent" (364).

In this occurrence of the first creation, the principle of light (understanding) and that of darkness (the ground) form themselves into the indivisible unity of a dynamic interaction in which God is constituted as "one" absolute existence (395), as the "supreme personality" (ibid.). God as the "absolute bond of both principles" (ibid.) is spirit "in the most eminent and absolute sense" (ibid.)—although precisely not as a pure spirit in an idealistic sense because God is the "living" unity of both powers and because he retains within himself his own "condition" (398), the "dark ground" of his existence (cf. 413). God as a person "is" the product of life and is, as such, the living unification of contradictory principles. Later we will show why and in which sense this conjunction of elements, which in themselves are heterogenous and separate, is the "mystery of love" (408, and below p. 74), and why on behalf of love God, who is "in himself," must become "for himself." We will show why he must become fully conscious, why he must attain "complete personification" (433), and why he decides to manifest and reveal himself in and through creation in order that love might reign.

First, however, it is important to see that, after God has created himself as a conscious personality due to the potency of his absolute freedom, he makes the "conscious and ethically free" (397ff.) decision for a world that is a deed of revelation, an expression of his living freedom. "Creation is not merely an event, it is a deed" (396). Its goal, then, cannot be "geometrically" deduced "from general laws." Furthermore, it cannot be a matter of God's "choosing" among a "plurality of possible worlds" or of "God's deliberating with himself" (ibid.). This "deed" is rather the realization of the divine essence that belongs to God's existence. This means that freedom, which is a consequence of this deed, is derived from the necessity contained in the laws of God's essence. In God, freedom and necessity are "identical." The original pattern for the world that is possible in accord with God's essence is the one that must come into existence (cf. 398). "In divine understanding itself, however, . . . there is only one God, just as there is only one possible world" (ibid.).

Does the difference between this conception and the traditional determinations of metaphysical necessity and freedom then, not suffice as an indication of the novelty of Schelling's attempt to redefine divine freedom in his *Inquiries*? In what sense is absolute, divine freedom determined differently in the *Inquiries*? In our analysis of the "leap" required in the "transition" of the divine essence from the nonground to "eternal oneness," it turned out that one determination of divine freedom consists in its "capability to initiate its own action," a determina-

tion that is similar to the traditional determination of finite human freedom, namely spontaneity. We then encountered a further determination
that resembles that of finite freedom. This determination is implied in
the voluntary commitment to the "necessity" of the law contained in
God's own nature—which is similar to the "*libertas determinationis*"
taken in its modern sense as a "self-determination."[21] The question
poses itself, however, whether it is not perhaps meaningless to speak of
self-determination if the divine "personality" has an autonomy that, although not opposed by any heteronomy, is infinitely superior to human,
finite autonomy? The difference in the determination of these two types
of freedom according to Schelling can presumably only be discovered
after we have seen how Schelling conceived of finite freedom in contrast
to absolute freedom. According to the title of the *Inquiries*, they are an
investigation into the essence of *human* freedom. This should be taken
as an indication that human freedom must first be understood before
one can understand the essence of God's absolute freedom.

IV

"GOD IS NOT a God of the dead, but of the living" (VII, 346). This
means that "God can only be revealed to himself in that which is similar
to him, in free beings that act on their own" (347). Only by proceeding
from the idea of "life" can we understand the character of self-revelation
and of that being which, because it is similar to God, plays the decisive
role in his self-revelation.

If the essence of the living God consists in his absolute freedom, then
the being that is similar to him must be "just as" free as God. Furthermore, this means that the "condition for the possibility" of this human
being's freedom must already be predisposed in the structure of divine
constitution. This is in fact true in a number of senses, as I intend
to show.

We have already seen that, in the form of the "divine vision of life,"
God remains present in the "ground" of his existence, which is constituted within him by being expelled through contraction. It is this presence in the "willing of the ground" (of "eternal longing") that now
makes possible the birth of human willing. "Man's will is the seed of
God, who is still present only in the ground, a seed concealed in eternal
longing; it is the divine vision of life enclosed in the depths, which God

espied when he resolved to will nature" (363). The "ground" is therefore not only the ground for God's existence, but also for creation, in particular for the will of that creature who is entrusted with a decisive role in God's self-revelation.

At first, however, the human will does not have its origin in divine existence, but rather in a principle that is independent within God. This means that the human will contains a "principle within itself that is independent in relation to God" (ibid.). The basic presupposition of self-revelation is thus preserved in that "the representations of the Godhead [can] only be independent beings" (347). In view of this postulated similarity, the fact that the human will contains a "principle which is independent in relation to God" implies even more. This independence implies that the free will is the will of a "being that is free, that acts on its own" (ibid.), a being that is autonomous and has a spiritual "selfness" or "personhood" (364), such as God. In its autonomy, this will is "similar" to God's absolute freedom. Although man is God's creation, something that has come to be through him, man is "derived" from God only "according to his becoming, not according to his Being: (346). This is true of every organic being. In this decisive passage, it becomes clear that Schelling's basic categories are conceived within the horizon of the concept of "life." It is no contradiction "that he who is a man's son is also a man" (ibid.). Man's freedom is therefore also "absolute or divine" just as God's is. Schelling stated, "The concept of derivative absoluteness of divinity contradicts itself so little that it is rather the mediating concept for all philosophy" (347).

But how does this finite and nevertheless absolute being complete its "absolute freedom?" Why is this completion given a decisive role within creation? Before these questions can be answered, we must examine the "conditions for the possibility" of finite freedom's constitution that are predisposed in divine nature.

Man—along with every other being that has come to be in nature—contains the ideal and the real principles within himself just as God does (cf. 362). To this extent, human nature finds itself in "the mere ground" (ibid.), in shadow and darkness, due to the real principle. The human being's willfullness [*Eigenwille*] is a "blind will"; it is "passion or desire" (363). Due to the ideal principle, which is a "principle of understanding," in man also, the dark principle is "transfigured into light" (ibid.). In man, this transfiguration is so complete that his particular will constitutes a "unified whole" together with the universal will, the will of understanding (ibid.). "Man contains the whole power of the dark principle and simultaneously the whole force of light. The deepest abyss and the highest heaven, both centers are contained in him" (ibid.).

Man's soul represents the "living" identity of both principles" (364). As the eternal spirit, God contains the living and indissoluable bond between both principles, as we have seen. Moreover, the "eternal spirit" possesses the word, *logos*. As mentioned earlier (cf. above p. 70) this word is expressed imperfectly in the things of nature; in man, however, it is perfectly expressed. For this reason the human soul as spirit possesses the divine word; that is, it is the abode in which God reveals himself as "actū existent" (364). The human spirit, which can make use of the divine word, is "in God" (410), and its freedom is therefore also in God (cf. below p. 78). But does such immanence not mean that the "absolute" freedom of man's will must be abandoned? If the human spirit is contained in God's, how can man play an autonomous role within the occurrence of self-revelation? The answer to this question characterizes Schelling's whole project, and thus the essence of divine freedom as opposed to finite freedom: God is a living God and his opposition belongs to his life. For this reason alone, it is impossible for the human spirit to be fully resolved into God's. God as a living God required a spirit that stands in opposition to him. We have seen that the divine spirit is the eternal bond between the real and the ideal forces (cf. VII, 373 and 430), that it is the unification of principles that in themselves are disparate and separate. This unification is an expression of God's love. His pure love strives to reveal itself, but this means that there must be something opposed to it outside of its own reality if it is to preserve itself in its purity. The opposite of pure love, however, is evil, and its reality outside of divine love lies in love's realization through finite, human freedom. If God has decided to reveal himself, if he requires self-revelation to be "for himself" [*für sich*] as a person in order not to be merely "in himself" [*an sich*]; then we can now see that he requires a being that is similar to himself and that possesses a freedom capable of good *and* evil. The human will cannot then find its expression in the merely formal concept of freedom as autonomy, as Kant and Idealism had thought, but is rather the "faculty for good and evil" (352). The fact that the two principles can be separated in the human spirit means that it is nothing other than the "possibility of good and evil" (364).

V

LET US NOW inquire more closely into the reality of evil, and in particular, into that freedom which is capable of evil, finite human freedom. As an "explanation" (375) of evil's reality, as an answer to the question of how it originated in created beings, Schelling remarks that for us "nothing is available other than the two principles in God," that is, nothing other than the conditions of possibility that are established in the theogony. The "will to evil," however, can be explained neither through the ideal principle nor through the determination of God as spirit, since the latter is "the purest love" (ibid.). Can the will to evil be explained through the real principle, the "will of the ground?" It turns out that this can be achieved only indirectly. If God's life is to reveal and thus realize itself as the purest love, something that strives counter to love [ein Widerstrebendes] must be found (376) that is predisposed in the "will of the ground" itself (cf. 375, 384). This must be conceived of in the following manner: The will of the ground arouses a "desire for that which is created" [Lust zum Kreatürlichen] and thus provokes evil "in general" (381) so that it attains self-consciousness in human volition (388). The will does this as a reaction to God's absolute freedom, to this order that is higher than everything created. It remains fundamentally true that, because evil is "also aroused" in the first creation through the reaction of the ground (381), because the created being has a will of its own, there is "a natural tendency toward evil in man" (ibid.). If man submits to this tendency, he has given the particular will, which originates in the ground, primacy over the universal will, which has its origins in the principle of light. He has "torn himself away" from the universal will (400). In either case, the two principles that are inseparably unified in the divine spirit are always separated in man. Man is able to separate them because his spirit is united with and carries within itself selfhood, which originates in the dark ground. In and of itself selfhood is not strictly evil. For when submissive, when it serves as a "basis," selfhood is the "keenness in life" [die Schärfe des Lebens] in which goodness becomes "receptive" [empfindlich] to itself (ibid.). "Anything good without effective selfhood is an ineffective good" (ibid.). Selfhood is spiritual and, as such, it is not only a unification of the ideal and real principles, of light and darkness; as personally spiritual it is "higher than the principle of light" (364). It is even capable of "elevating itself above nature" and thus becoming "the will which beholds itself in complete freedom" (ibid.). This means that on the one hand, personally spiritual selfhood has the principles at its disposal and, on the other hand, that it is placed in the position of decision making: man decides to be good or evil.

The separation of those principles that are inseparable in God leads to the elevation of the particular will over the universal will: precisely this is the realization of evil. A will that, as a universal will, particularizes itself has reversed the proper relationship. This "reversal" [*Umkehrung*] must be understood "ontologically." It does not refer to a "moral" decision in a narrow sense, but to a decision concerning a way "to be." In evil, a decision is made to form an inverse unity directed against the whole. In this sense, Schelling called this "reversal" of principles an "inverse God" [*umgekehrten Gott*] (390).

Whenever man employs spiritual selfhood not as an instrument but instead allows it to predominate, derangement arises—a "false life, a life of lies, a growth of restlessness and corruption" (366). Whenever man has rent asunder the divine bond of forces within himself, then the "hunger of a craving for self" (390) arises within him, and "he falls from the arrogance of being everything into non-Being" (391). He has then touched on the ground of creation and profaned the mystery. Even if he has thereby lost his initial freedom (391–92), there is still a "life" in this mode of Being, for man cannot fully abolish the original (divine) bond of forces (366). Human freedom, even when it has taken evil as its determination, maintains a *relationship* to the divine condition since this condition is the absolute condition of all spiritual Being.

We now return to our original question: What is Schelling's concept of finite human freedom? In accordance with Kant's concept of freedom, he proceeded from the assumption that the freedom of man's actions occurs beyond the world of appearance, that man's freedom is supratemporal and is not subject to the causality of nature. "Free actions immediately result out of that which is intelligible in man" (384). Thus, for Schelling just as for Kant, man's freedom of action is a self-determination of which man is capable due to his noumenal essence.

Furthermore, according to Kant a rational being can also *fail* to exercise rational moral self-determination, it can *refuse* to adopt the universal law as a maxim for its will. For Kant, as Schelling interpreted him, man is essentially characterized by indecisiveness; man's freedom is "voluntary choice" [*Willkür*]. For Schelling, by contrast, the intelligible deed of self-determination occurs together with the "first creation." This means that it is an eternal deed outside of time (386) in the same sense in which the original deed of creation through God's contracting himself is eternal and outside of time. The original deed of creation posits "only a beginning *of* time, and not a beginning *in* time" (cf. 430). Similarly, man's intelligible deed is not a "beginning in time" so that it would be the first of a series of discrete actions following one after the other and developing in time (cf. ibid.). It is rather an "eternal beginning" [*ewiger Anfang*] (386) for all of the singular actions that occur in time; it is the principle "which throughout all time" (385–86) constitutes the unity of their determinations. This unity must "always be completely and perfectly present in advance . . . so that a singular action or determination within it is possible" (383–84). Self-determination in regard to singular actions can thus only mean that man follows the laws of his own essence, and that means of his own character (cf. 430), which he has determined in the "first creation." The freedom of his singular actions, therefore, consists in the necessity of the character that he has decided on, one way or the other. This necessity is a *beata necessitas*, a "holy necessity" (391), and is not to be confused with the modal category of necessity that applies to natural beings. Neither does the essence (the determinations) precede freedom, nor does freedom precede the determinations. Fichte correctly described this point of their unification by means of the notion of an "active deed" [*Tathandlung*] (385). This "active deed" is simultaneously freedom and determinacy (necessity), neither of the two can be derived from the other. The free deed does not result from the essence, since the latter is only present with the former; nor does the essence result from the free deed, because something determinate cannot result from something indeterminate. The full concept of freedom (which includes necessity) is therefore "a real self-positing" [*ein reales Selbstsetzen*], and human freedom must therefore also be thought of in relation to good and evil (cf. below p. 78). This sense of an active deed [22] refers to an identity between necessity and freedom, a noumenal existence above all creation (364), which is valid only for the essence of man and only appears when man acts in accordance with his essence. In this vein, it is stated that, "The essence of man is essentially *his own deed*" (384).

In contrast to Kant's determination of "radical evil," according to which man is still able to "predominate" over evil,[23] Schelling saw the crucial decision as having been made once and for all "in the original active deed." Through this deed, he wrote, "man's life extends back to the beginning of creation, since by means of it he is . . . free and himself an eternal beginning" (386). Every man thus has a feeling that corresponds to this idea "as if he has been what he is for all eternity and by no means merely became so in time" (ibid.).

Reservations against accepting this interpretation of Schelling's concept of finite freedom are prompted by the fact that Schelling intended to overcome the "formal concept of freedom" precisely by means of a "real and living concept," which he recognized to be "a faculty of good and evil" (352). This latter determination of freedom, moreover, appears to be nothing other than freedom of choice with regard to singular actions. In the passage previously quoted, however, Schelling did not speak of a "faculty for good *or* evil." He explicitly referred instead to a faculty for good *and* evil. The formal concept of freedom is *not* concretized as a kind of "willful choice," as a freedom of choice with regard to specific actions. Rather, the reality of evil and its realization through man are thought of as being essentially entailed in the concept of freedom. Evil is necessary in the plan of creation: it is necessary that there be a finite freedom that makes a decision for and realizes evil. The reality of evil and its realization are also just as unconditionally necessary for the beginning of creation as they are for creation's "ultimate intention" (404). The "complete actualization of God" (ibid.), and thus the universal reign of his love (ibid.), presupposes that finite freedom must espouse evil in order for goodness to be able to emerge as having been purified from evil. Only by way of evil and its having been overcome can good be separated from evil so that evil is in the end "eternally relegated to non-Being" (ibid.), and the way is thus opened for the exclusive reign of God's love. The separation of good from evil, this "crisis" (ibid.), indeed presupposes the "ground" that solicits evil; however, Schelling's theodicy is unique in that the "ground" is not in itself evil (400).

The role that finite freedom plays in the event of creation can now be more precisely determined. We have seen that man is independent in his Being, that he has an "inner independence from God" and a "freedom in regard to God" (cf. above pp. 00ff. and VII, 458). Man is descended from the ground, and thus from a principle that is independent of God. Furthermore, this independence and this self-sufficiency are most clearly expressed in the fact that man possesses a faculty that in its essence is not derived from God—a faculty for evil. On the other hand, man's will is nevertheless predisposed as a "seed" in the divine vision of life (cf. above p. 72). This is man's initial "Being in God" (cf. above p. 74), and as a finite spirit man is contained in the "divine spirit" (411). Schelling states explicitly that only through "Being in God . . . is man capable of freedom" (ibid.). Human freedom is finite above all because it serves God. As we have seen, God's love can only reign if goodness has constituted itself by overcoming evil, and this means that man *must* decide on evil in order to assist the triumph of goodness and, along with it, the complete reign of divine love. This means that finite freedom has its end, its boundary, in the *telos* of the process as a whole, in the "ultimate intention" of divine creation (404).

It becomes obvious at this point that Schelling comprehended the whole occurrence—God's life, God's absolute freedom, creation, and finite freedom—within a framework based on the concepts of *telos* and *entelechia*. Nevertheless, the "teleology" of this occurrence is not oriented toward the model of a Greek doctrine of substance, toward an "ousiology." This occurrence does not proceed to its end circularly and blindly in the way that *Uranos*, the heavens, proceeds to its inherent "end." This occurrence is rather a history of salvation (cf. 379) influenced by monotheism, messianism, and Christology; a history oriented toward a future event of salvation, toward God's completely conscious self-realization. Man's finite freedom in his relationship to evil is determined in reference to this occurrence as a whole: man's independence and self-sufficiency in relation to God, man's "derivative absoluteness," is tied to the ultimate intention of divine creation. For this reason, finite freedom *must* espouse evil; it *must* become entangled in evil; and, for this reason, finite freedom can and must, with divine assistance, decide "to die to this world of senses" (VI, 53, cf. VII, 405–406) and to let "the ground be effective within it" (VI, 375). It is necessary for the good principle "to be allowed to be active within it [i.e. freedom]" (389) so that evil may be relegated to "complete irreality" (405). This "return" to the absolute principle that is actively accomplished by finite freedom must take place in order that the complete reign of divine love may be achieved.

Human freedom is furthermore determined by its position in relation to nature. This position can likewise only be understood against the background of Schelling's eschatological conception as a whole. Insofar as man originates from the ground, he has "roots in nature" that are independent of God (cf. 458). He is nevertheless free from nature insofar as he stands "above nature in the midst of nature" (ibid.). For, he not only has a "soul," as does every other living being; he also has a spirit. Through his freedom from nature and through his spiritual essence, man is predestined to be the "mediator" between God and nature (411). "Placed in the point of indifference" (458), man is the being in whom the divine word is completely expressed. Man is the being capable of *logos*, of rational speech, which is why he can take on himself the task of being "nature's redeemer" (411). He can spiritualize nature by explaining the "archetypes" [*Vorbilder*], which are directed toward him as "anticipations" [*Vorbedeutungen*] in nature (415). Schelling's early philosophy of nature had demonstrated how nature in its spiritual permeation, in the disclosure of its egolike, volitional, dynamic, and free essence, proves itself to be akin and even identical to the human spirit. The *Inquiries* does not merely seek to overcome this dichotomy within the sphere of finitude: "Since he himself is bound to God" (411), man, in his efforts to recognize nature's lawfulness actively assists in the process by which "God accepts nature and transforms it into himself" (ibid.).

At the beginning of this study, we saw that Schelling's transcendental philosophy and his philosophy of nature had demonstrated an identity within the finite realm by proceeding from the concept of finite freedom. The question then arose whether it had been the task of the *Inquiries* to prove that this dimension is in turn grounded in an absolute. We have since seen that, within the finite dimension, the finite human spirit serves the teleological occurrence, the ultimate intention of divine creation, in a twofold sense: first of all, by espousing evil in order to enable goodness and, in the end, the complete reign of love to be victorious; and secondly, by spiritualizing nature, so that nature in this form can return to the divine spirit. In this active movement, which human freedom performs in returning from evil to the love of God and which nature undergoes in returning to spirit, a side of the dynamic occurrence shows itself in which the dimension of finitude is grounded in that infinitude, in God's absolute freedom. We must, however, still ask how this occurrence appears from the other side. How does God's absolute freedom realize the grounding of finite freedom within itself?

In the preface to the *Phenomenology of Spirit*, Hegel remarked in criticism of Schelling: "God's life and divine knowledge may therefore very well be expressed as a play of love with itself: This idea sinks to edification and even to triteness if the seriousness, the pain, the patience, and the labor of negativity are lacking therein" (*PhG*, 20, *10*).

We have seen that, for Schelling, the determination "life" had the same implications that the determination "negativity" had for Hegel: an internal self-movement that posits itself in opposition, in dissimilarity, in order to find its way back to itself by proceeding out of this opposition into identity. For Schelling, the issue was not the life of "the concept" (ibid., 44, *33–34*) or its self-determination in generating the "complete wealth of its developed form" (ibid. 21, *11*), as it had been for Hegel. Nonetheless, Schelling did view life as a process that is characterized by its "fluidity" (ibid. 135ff., *106ff.*). Furthermore, regarding the "seriousness," "pain," and "labor" of life, it must be noted that the force that they have in furthering the affirmative powers is greatly surpassed by the force of evil. For, God in his infinite freedom makes himself into the ground of finite freedom without encroaching on its autonomy. He accomplishes this by utilizing finite freedom and allowing it in the struggle with evil to experience its "fate," which is "subject to suffering and becoming" (cf. VII, 403). Only through the temptation that evil arouses ever anew does the "inner fluidity," which Hegel spoke of, come about at all; for, only through this temptation is the rigidity dissolved within the realm of morality. Only by means of this temptation can the constantly renewed struggle be provoked in which finite freedom seeks goodness over and over again. This is the only way in which, with the help of God's grace, the "death" (cf. 405–406) of evil desires can be achieved so that the rebirth can occur, which is a necessary preparation for the exclusive reign of divine love. This fate, this finite struggle for goodness, encompasses the whole realm of morality and transforms it through and through. This complete realization by way of the tragedy of finite freedom's entanglement in evil is anything but a "play of love" of God with himself. In truth, it is the genuine conception of the way in which finitude is grounded in infinity; it is a realization of "ethics" [*Sittlichkeit*] (VI, 53).

If we observe both sides of the dynamic occurrence of grounding, we recognize something new and unique in Schelling's *Philosophical Inquiries* and in its principal conclusions. God's infinite freedom, his infinite will, the primal Being, realizes itself only in cooperation with finite freedom, finite willing. Through the concept of "cooperation" [*Mitwirken*], the essence not only of divine freedom, but also that of finite freedom are completely transformed. The latter no longer denotes the "good will" of a rational being that subjects itself to its own moral legislation (Kant), nor is it understood in the sense implied in a "will which is in and for itself" and which realizes itself in an ethical order manifested by good laws and civil institutions because the individual rediscovers himself in them (Hegel).[24] The finite will, finite freedom, finds its true essence by relinquishing the connotations implied in such subjectivity and becoming an active collaborator in the play of the realization of divine love. Infinite, divine, absolute freedom thus in turn attains its true essence and proves itself to be of such a nature that it limits its absoluteness on its own, i.e., "contracts it," in order to enable finite freedom to come to play as well. This insight into the "interwovenness" [*Verschränkung*] of absolute and finite freedom, this formulation of the grounding occurrence, is in my view the speculative achievement in Schelling's thought.

In the *System of Transcendental Idealism*, Schelling had already conceived of the finite spirit's collaboration by employing the image of "One Spirit that acts as poetic author in all spirits" (III, 602). The poet "is" in the grand play of a gradually self-manifesting revelation. Here God is revealed and discloses himself gradually in the play of our freedom so that without this freedom "he himself *would not be*." In the finitude of our own freedom, we are not only "poetic coauthors of the whole," we are even "self-improvisors of the particular roles which we play" (ibid.).

Although even at that stage Schelling had already envisaged the image of a "mutual belonging" [*Zusammengehörigkeit*] between absolute and finite freedom, he had not been able to grasp this relationship *in conceptual terms* (cf. above, p. 18). The *Inquiries*, however, conceives of the relationship between infinite freedom and finite freedom by disclosing both of them in their active realization through evil. In so doing, the *Inquiries* responded to the "need of philosophy" at that time. For, here the concept of freedom, which Transcendental Philosophy and the Philosophy of Nature had synthesized into a system of finitude, is "grounded" in absolute freedom. In this "grounding," the absolute as infinity in the end transforms finitude into absoluteness, into the ele-

ment proper to it (cf. VII, 423). That which is to be transformed, however, is also for its part active in this transformation. The truth is thus
grounded in an eschatological event so that that which is "supreme"
and "was already present before creation was present" (406) finally
emerges as the dimension that makes possible the beginning, the "initial nonground," God's absolute freedom. This dimension, therefore,
appears as "the general unity that is the same toward all, but captive to
none: [as] the beneficience that is free from all else but permeates everything; in a word, [as] love, which is all in all" (408–409).[25]

Appendix

THE DISTINCTION between cosmogony and theogony in Schelling's
middle period may seem problematic and requires further explanation.
In a certain sense, the problem involved in this distinction touches on
the foundations of his system, insofar as it is thought of as overcoming
the (false) alternative between theism and pantheism. According to the
pantheistic view, the difference between God and the world, and thus,
along with it, between theogony and cosmogony, had been completely
abolished. According to the theistic view, the difference was posited absolutely—God as a completed, eternal being was set in opposition to
the world; and, at the very most, the question concerning creation arose
independently of the question concerning God's Being in himself.
Schelling can be viewed as espousing a conception of the absolute that
supercedes both of these views insofar as he tried to conceive of the absolute with regard to its own self-revelation. The conditions of this self-
revelation are at the same time the conditions of the existence of that
which is other than the absolute (of nature, of the "world"). This is precisely the problem involved in this distinction: Through the separation
of principles within itself, the absolute posits itself as an (ideal) being
and its opposite, Being (i.e., a "relative" [*beziehungsweise*] nonbeing,
that which is real, $A = B$). Is this absolute, which is identical with its
self-positing, likewise at one with that which, in the sense of creation,
posits something other than itself as a self-sufficient existence? Or is a
further, independent decision to proceed to creation required? The
question is complicated by the additional problem that for Schelling
one can speak of the absolute, God, in a number of ways. Taken as the
absolute purely for itself before the separation of the principles (into the

"powers" [*Potenzen*]), the absolute appears as "that which is above beings," as the "primal ground," the "nonground," or "indifference." After
this separation, it appears as a being (existence) in opposition to the
ground (its Being). Furthermore, from the vantage point of the first absolute, it appears as the ground itself. The absolute (in the first sense)
posits—or rather must posit—itself as the ground in order (by negat-
ing the simultaneity within it) to be able to initiate the continuing series
of powers.[26] It should be added that after the separation, the absolute
also appears in the third power as the unity of the first and second powers, as the completely disclosed unity of the absolute subsequent to its
separation (cf. VII, 427).

In view of the *Inquiries*, one must ask how we can incorporate the
concept of God's personality into this general scheme. Here personality
(with regard to God) is the indissoluable bond between ideality and reality. This is not, however, to be confused with the third power, since
only the third power is the final unity between God and creation as the
"love that is all in all." The third power is the last period of God's self-
revelation. Thus God must first of all be able to emerge as a person, for
it is as love, the affirmative principle, the ideal that he is, that he posits
himself for himself. (In the *Stuttgart Private Lectures*, and even more
clearly in *The Ages of the World*, the doctrine of principles is increasingly resolved into the simple opposition between two principles. In the
Inquiries it appears in a much more differentiated manner.) This self-
positing is furthermore accompanied by, and made possible through, an
expulsion of that principle that is opposed to God's essence as love: egoism. It is through the expulsion of the negative principle (egoism) that
the affirmative principle is made into the ground of God's revelation. In
this sense, God becomes manifest himself by first positing himself as
affirmation in relation to his negation and by then becoming conscious
of himself. (This relationship appears as the relationship of beings to
Being, or of subject to predicate in the *Stuttgart Private Lectures* and in
The Ages of the World; in the *Inquiries* it appears as the relationship between existence and ground.) Must an independent act of revelation be
conceived of in addition to this constitution of God as a being [*eines
seienden Gottes*] in order that creation may occur? Or does the self-
revelation of the absolute (as indifference) also imply the creation of the
world merely due to the fact that, in its self-revelation, the absolute
freely limits itself and posits a ground? Although some of Schelling's

statements can be interpreted in this direction, creation in the proper sense must nevertheless be distinguished from the theogonic process of God's coming into being, both with regard to the concept and to the matter of concern itself. For creation does not properly consist in excluding from God that darkness that is in him (this is the way in which the "theogonic" process occurs). Rather, one can speak properly of creation only if that which is excluded proceeds to be developed into something higher, if divinity enclosed within itself (the first power) is actualized and raised to clarity (cf. 434: "creation therefore consists in producing something higher, something properly divine, in that which is excluded."). Precisely because the separation into a conscious part of God (which is God "*sensu eminenti*" 435) and an "unconscious" part would contradict his love (i.e. God's essence as having become "for itself"), a creation is required in which this love may communicate itself. Creation is *not* required in order that God may become "actual." God's relationship to nature, in which he produces that which is higher, is one of actuality to potentiality; and the expansion of "divinity" into nature (the awakening of the "divine vision of life") already presupposes God in his actuality. (Cf. 441: "nature is therefore divine, but a lower kind of divinity, a divinity that is awakened from death, so to speak, a divinity that has been elevated from non-Being into Being—whereby it still remains distinct from the most initial divinity that does not have to be first awakened from non-Being to Being.")

NOTES

1. Basic Notions in Schelling's and Habermas's Conceptions of History

1. Cf. W. Marx, *Reason and World: Between Tradition and a New Beginning* (The Hague, 1971), preface.

2. Regarding the thesis that, and how, the younger Hegel was influenced by basic ideas from Greek philosophy during the Jena period that he shared with Schelling, see W. Marx, "The Meaning and Task of Philosophy in German Idealism," *Reason and World*, pp. 1ff.

3. Cf. W. Marx, *The Meaning of Aristotle's Ontology* (The Hague, 1954), pp. 57ff.; and *Introduction to Aristotle's Theory of Being as Being* (The Hague, 1977), pp. 38ff.

4. Schelling, *Darstellung meines Systems der Philosophie* (1801), IV, p. 26.

5. Cf. W. Marx, *Aristotle's Theory*, pp. ixf.

6. This notion plays an important role in a number of Löwith's works concerning the history of thought; cf. especially *Weltgeschichte und Heilsgeschehen* (Stuttgart, 1953).

7. Cf. G. W. F. Hegel, *Vorlesungen über die Philosophie der Weltgeschichte*, 11:27, [English: *Reason in History*, trans. R. Hartmann (Indianapolis, 1953), p. 27.]

8. Jürgen Habermas, *Das Absolute und die Geschichte von der Zwiespältigkeit in Schelling's Denken* (Ph.D. dissertation, University of Frankfurt, 1954); "Dialektischer Idealismus im Übergang zum Materialismus—Geschichtsphilosophische Folgerungen aus Schellings Idee einer Contraction Gottes," in *Theorie und Praxis* (Frankfurt, 1971), pp. 172ff.

9. Habermas, *Erkenntnis und Interesse*, mit einem neuen Nachwort (Frankfurt, 1973), pp. 38f., *26* [The page number printed in italics refers to the English translation, *Knowledge and Human Interest*, trans. Jeremy Shapiro (Boston, 1969). In all subsequent citations, this work will be referred to by its English title, the first page mentioned will refer to the German edition of 1973, and the following italicized page number will refer to Shapiro's translation.]

10. Habermas, *Technik und Wissenschaft als Ideologie* (Frankfurt, 1969), p. 160.

11. *Knowledge and Human Interest*, p. 38, *26*.

12. To judge from the appendix to the new edition of *Knowledge and Human Interest*, Habermas himself seemed to consider his attempt to comprehend the species' history both as a history of transcendental consciousness and as a continuation of the evolution of nature in a materialistic vein to be inadequate. The "empirical" status of cognitive interests in their transcendental function is supposed to be understood "in quotation marks" since a theory of evolution that would undertake to explain transcendental frameworks "materialistically" cannot in turn be developed within a transcendental framework of objectifying sciences (*Knowledge and Human Interest*, p. 410; cf. also the preface to the new

edition of *Theorie und Praxis*, p. 28). Even if the meaning of this unusual mediation between empirical and transcendental determinations could be clarified, the question would still remain, how one can resolve the conception of the species' history as a "history of transcendental consciousness" (*Knowledge and Human Interest*, p. 58, *41*) with the supposition that the transcendental framework of instrumental action is the result of an evolution in nature that precedes this history and is thus invariable in the historical development of the socio-cultural being "man" (cf. ibid., p. 48, *35*, 57, *41*; *400*).

13. *Technik und Wissenschaft*, p. 160.

14. This remains true even though Habermas distanced himself somewhat from his orientation on the "traditional linguistic usage of 'reflection' that is derived from German Idealism" in the appendix to the new edition of *Knowledge and Human Interest*. There, he distinguished between reflection as reconstruction and reflection as self-critique, both of which find their justification in the concept of reflection developed in German Idealism, where they are, however, "confused with each other." This distinction does not affect our argument, since we are concerned primarily with reflection as self-critique. Its determination remains unchanged, and in this appendix Habermas has by no means restricted its "power." Reflection as self-critique remains for him an "analytical liberation from objective illusions," i.e. not from structures of experience that are intersubjective constants and are unmasked by reflection as reconstruction, but rather from "self-generated pseudo-objectivity" (ibid., *1412*). One of its essential marks of distinction as opposed to reflection as reconstruction lies in the fact that it has "practical consequences." It thus appears to be a stimulus to consciousness and an alteration at the same time (cf. note 37).

15. *Knowledge and Human Interest*, p. 60, *43*.

16. Habermas's critical discussion of Theunissen's and of Rohrmoser's critiques of "naturalism" in critical theory also bears witness to his distance from traditional Marxist materialism. At the same time, the formulation of the "highly unnatural idea of truth" as the "possibility of universal communication" and as a "fact of nature" demonstrates the dilemma in which Habermas is caught due to his orientation on both Marx and German Idealism (ibid. pp. 415f.).

17. I. Kant, *Grundlegung zur Metaphysik der Sitten*, in *Kants Gesammelte Schriften* (Berlin, 1902), 4:447ff. (English translation available in various editions.)

18. Habermas, *Technik und Wissenschaft*, p. 164.

19. Cf. *Knowledge and Human Interest*, p. 350, *286*.

20. *Technik und Wissenschaft*, p. 68.

21. In his 1968 essay on Technology, Habermas reconstructed the thresholds of the species' history under the obvious influence of Marx's dialectics between the productive forces and the conditions of production. Habermas was here convinced that "from the outset the mechanism of the species' development" consists in the fact that "under the pressure of relatively developed productive forces, a structural transformation is compelled to take place in the institutional framework" (*Technik und Wissenschaft*, p. 68). Nevertheless, he granted that this mechanism alone does not determine the further course of history, e.g. it does not sufficiently explain how capitalism arose on the basis of a

traditional society. The conclusion of the essay justifies the conjecture that he also seemed to grant critical reflection a creative power.

22. *Knowledge and Human Interest*, p. 85, *62*. It must be noted that Habermas also employed the model of a dialectic of ethics taken from Hegel's early theological writings. Cf. pp. 77ff., *56ff*.; and *Nachwort zu Hegels politischen Schriften* (Frankfurt, 1966), p. 355. We shall not pursue this point in view of the declaration that "social theory remains in the framework of the *Phenomenology*" (*Knowledge and Human Interest*, p. 85, *62*).

23. Cf. W. Marx, *Hegel's Phenomenology of Spirit* (New York, 1975), pp. 51ff.

24. Hegel, *Phänomenologie des Geistes* (Hamburg, 1952) p. 69, *51*. [The italicized numeral refers to the English translation by A. V. Miller (Oxford, 1977).]

25. Cf. W. Marx, *Hegel's Phenomenology*, pp. 7, 15ff.

26. Cf. especially regarding this point: Rüdiger Bubner, "Was ist kritische Theorie?" in *Hermeneutik und Ideologiekritik* (Frankfurt, 1971), pp. 160ff.

27. *Knowledge and Human Interest*, p. 83, *61*.

28. Hegel, *Phänomenologie*, p. 69, *51*.

29. *Knowledge and Human Interest*, p. 83, *61*.

30. The most important guideline for reflecting on "reconstruction" in Habermas's social theory is that, in addition to the "technical" interest guiding knowledge and the "practical" interest involved in it, there is an "emancipatory" interest that drives society to dissolve the compulsion existing in society. For an explanation of the "inducement" [*Auslösung*] of reflection, however, Habermas did not invoke this interest.

31. Cf. W. Marx, *Hegel's Phenomenology*, pp. 78ff.

32. Hegel, *Phänomenologie*, p. 71, *53*.

33. *Knowledge and Human Interest*, p. 9, *vii*.

34. Hegel, *Phänomenologie*, p. 73, *55*.

35. His orientation toward Hegel's determination and employment of reflection in the *Phenomenology* is expressly reiterated in the appendix to the new edition of *Knowledge and Human Interest*, p. 412.

36. *Knowledge and Human Interest*, p. 342, *281*.

37. Although, in his most recent publications, Habermas maintained his conviction that self-reflection determined after the model of a therapeutic conversation has "a wealth of practical consequences," he seemed to lean toward a more cautious estimation of the power that enlightenment has to change things. This is partially due to Gadamer's criticism. In any case, in Habermas's discussion with critics of the psychoanalytical model (in the preface to the new edition of *Theorie und Praxis*, cf. also pp. 36f.), he clearly distinguished between the "formation and further development of critical theorems," the "organization of enlightenment processes," and an "engagement in political conflict" (ibid. p. 37).

38. Translator's note: The German term *Aufhebung* (along with *aufheben* and *aufgehoben*) as employed by Hegel and others in German Idealism entails a threefold movement involving the negation, conservation, and elevation of the object concerned. There is no term in the English language that adequately expresses all three of these aspects of *Aufhebung*, so I have in each particular

case chosen the expression that, in my opinion, most nearly approximates the single aspect that is predominant in that context. Nevertheless, wherever the term *Aufhebung* is used in a strict sense, all three aspects should be implicitly understood. The German term has often been cited in parentheses in order to facilitate this understanding.

39. This essay deals only with those aspects of Habermas's conception that appear to us to be relevant for his "theory of history" (as presented above all in his major work *Knowledge and Human Interest* and in his inaugural lecture with the same title). We have not taken into account his central thesis concerning a theory of science. According to this thesis, the meaning of the validity of empirical and analytical sciences as well as of the hermeneutic sciences of culture is founded on the interests that guide our knowledge and constitute these objective realms. These are in turn said to be founded on the life-world of labor, the functional horizon for instrumental activity, or on the life-world community of communication partners, which generates intersubjectivity in the form of interaction and practical and theoretical discourse. The more recent publications regarding a theory of language were dealt with only in regard to their relevance for his theory of history.

40. Cf. Habermas, *Theorie der Gesellschaft oder Sozialtechnologie* (Frankfurt, 1972), p. 139.

41. Habermas, *Legitimationsprobleme im Spätkapitalismus* (Frankfurt, 1973), pp. 19ff.

2. The Task and Method of Philosophy in Schelling's
System of Transcendental Idealism and in Hegel's
Phenomenology of Spirit

1. Cf. W. Marx, "The Meaning and Task of Philosophy in German Idealism" in *Reason and World* (The Hague, 1971) pp. 1ff.

2. Translator's note: Regarding the threefold meaning of *Aufhebung*, see above p. 89, note 38.

3. Cf. Klaus Düsing, "Speculation and Reflection. Zur Zusammenarbeit Schellings und Hegels in Jena," *Hegel-Studien* 5 (1969) pp. 95ff.

4. Cf. M. Frank, *Der unendliche Mangel an Sein* (Frankfurt, 1975). Frank also emphasized the aspect of "prereflectivity," especially in recourse to Sartre.

5. Cf. on this point: Adolf Schurr, *Philosophie als System bei Fichte, Schelling und Hegel* (Stuttgart, 1974).

6. In Fichte's *Wissenschaftslehre*, opposition is by no means implied in the nondeducible principle of positing oneself, nor can it be deduced from that principle. If that were the case, then, as Fichte declared, the ego would suspend itself [*sich aufheben*]. Cf. Fichte, *Werke*, Gesamtausgabe der Bayerischen Akademie der Wissenschaften, ed. R. Lauth and H. Jacobs, Vol. I, 2 (Stuttgart-Bad Canstatt, 1965), pp. 381f. In contrast to this, according to Schelling, "the concept of positing an opposite necessarily must be conceived of in terms of the concept of positing." As we have emphasized, Schelling viewed the intellectual intuition as "absolute identity" and thus as the original and immediate pure realization of a self-positing into an intuiting agent and the object of intuition, into producer and product. The ego must, however, simultaneously posit itself such that "the other," its "opposition," can become its object. Pure self-

consciousness cannot, therefore, be identical through and through, it must be "simultaneously identical and synthetic" (ibid.). The "One Act" of self-consciousness is "absolute synthesis," a synthesis of ideal and real activities that is derived from an "original duplicity." If this synthesis of activities is represented by the transcendental philosopher as arising successively, then it becomes evident that these activities are the conditions for an identity of self-consciousness that is then "not an original identity, but rather a mediated and generated identity" (392–93).

7. Cf. on this point: Dieter Jähnig, *Die Kunst in der Philosophie* Vol. 1, *Schellings Begründung von Natur und Geschichte* (Pfullingen, 1966), p. 113, pp. 127ff; Vol. 2 *Die Wahrheitsfunktion der Kunst* (Pfullingen, 1969), pp. 285ff.

8. Ibid.

9. See, for example, Walter Schulz's introduction to *System des tranzcendentalen Idealismus* (Hamburg, 1957), pp. xxviff.; Dieter Jähnig, *Die Kunst in der Philosophie*, pp. 133ff. and 155ff.

10. Cf. concerning the following: W. Marx, *Hegel's Phenomenology of Spirit* (New York, 1975).

11. *Vorlesungen über die Geschichte der Philosophie*, 15, p. 655.

12. Cf. note 10.

13. Cf. concerning this point: W. Marx, "Die Dialektik und die Rolle des Phenomenologen," *Hegel-Jahrbuch* (1974): 381–87.

14. Richard Kroner, *Von Kant bis Hegel* (Tübingen, 1924), p. 110.

15. Walter Schulz, *Die Vollendung des Deutschen Idealismus in der Spätphilosophie Schellings* (Stuttgart, 1955), p. 132.

16. Ibid., p. 135.

17. Habermas, for example; cf. the first essay in this book.

3. The Task of Schelling's *Philosophical Inquiries into the Essence of Human Freedom*

1. Cf. I, pp. 174ff.; cf. also W. Marx, "The Meaning and Task of Philosophy in German Idealism," in *Reason and World* (The Hague, 1971); and W. Marx, "Vom Bedürfnis der Philosophie," in *Von der Notwendigkeit der Philosophie in der Gegenwart, Festschrift für Karl Ulmer zum 60. Geburtstag*, ed. Helmut Kohlenberger and Wilhelm Lütterfelds (Munich, 1976).

2. Cf. above p. 89, note 38.

3. In the *Ideas Concerning a Philosophy of Nature* (1797), the *World Soul* (1798), and the *First Draft of a System of the Philosophy of Nature* (1800).

4. Translator's note: The distinction between "*Sein*," "*Seiendes*," or "*Seiendsein*," and "*Wesen*" is very important in the *Inquiries* in particular, and for Schelling's later philosophy as a whole. In this essay, I have therefore introduced the term "Being" (always capitalized) to refer to the German term "*Sein*." The term "being" (not capitalized) is used by contrast, to render the German term "*seiend*" or "*ein Seiendes*." In reference to God, I have consistently translated the term "*Wesen*" as "essence" even in contexts in which this may not correspond completely to the normal use of the term. In reference to man, I have, however, translated the term "*Wesen*" as "being" (e.g. "the human being") except in cases where the connotation of an inherent characteristic is implied, so that the use of the term "essence" or "essential" is demanded.

5. Cf. on this point: W. Marx, *The Meaning of Aristotle's Ontology* (The Hague, 1954), pp. 62ff.; and W. Marx, *Introduction to Aristotle's Theory of Being* (The Hague, 1977), pp. 43ff.

6. In the treatise *Philosophie und Religion*, which appeared in 1804 and can be seen as the transition from the phase of the System of Identity to Schelling's "middle period" (cf. on this point: Harold Holz, *Spekulation und Faktizität* [Bonn, 1970], pp. 41ff., in particular his discussion with Fuhrman in the passage quoted and in note 1), Schelling rejected the possibility of a "negative" approach to the absolute, in which the absolute would be thought of in opposition to that which is not absolute (VI, 21). For, then the absolute would be caught up in a dependence on that which is not absolute (22). It would be just as wrong to construct the absolute from a relationship of moments (subject-object) that constitute its identity. Without a conceptual mediation, an appropriate grasp of the absolute is possible only in "intellectual intuition" (cf. 26, 29f.), as we have already seen in his conception of the *System of Transcendental Idealism* (see above, the two preceding essays). Schelling's reasons for the rejection of mediating reflection in regard to the absolute "in itself" are based on the fact that, for him, the absolute is not "composite" but rather "simple" (26) and without mediation, so that it is therefore immediately comprehensible (31). The absolute is held to be an "idea" [*Idee*] that has come alive (27); and it is thus not a conceptual unity (cf. 29f.), but rather, as a living unity, it is an immediate unity of its oppositions. Reflection makes the mistake of trying to explain it by means of various constructions of the relationship of these oppositions, but this approach cannot fail to miss the immediacy of this living unity, since it can only be recognized in intuition. The absolute as a living unity is infinitely more than could be expressed by its determination as a conceptual unity.

7. "I have always represented that which I called Philosophy of Nature and Transcendental Philosophy as opposing poles in philosophizing; in this presentation I am situated at the point of indifference . . ." (IV, 108).

8. "That life which the beings within the all have in relation to one another is opposed to their life in God, in which each of them is free and itself infinite; to this extent, it is their life which is separated and fallen from God" (VII, 190).

9. Harold Holz, *Spekulation und Faktizität*, by contrast, tried to show that the influence of the theosophists—in opposition to the widespread opinion expressed in scholarly literature on Schelling—either did not exist or had only a subordinate significance (cf. § 1). Holz viewed Neo-Platonic influences as the truly decisive influences on Schelling. We can no more consent to Holz's thesis in its fundamental generality than to those theses that reduce Schelling's philosophy of freedom to theosophic thought. Neither can one doubt the effect of theosophic influences on Schelling, nor can it be denied that he also adopted Neo-Platonic themes in his thought, especially since the theosophic tradition cannot in turn be conceived of without Neo-Platonism. The mutual exclusion of these traditions must be ruled out from the very beginning. In the end, all research into common motifs finds its limits in the fact that every independent thinker transforms the motifs that he adopts according to his own fundamental question, and he never simply reproduces a traditional doctrine. With Schelling, this is especially true. Schelling's basic concept of freedom could not simply fall back behind the concept of freedom which had been attained in Idealism (cf. *Inquiries*, VII, 383; see above pp. 61–62).

In *Platonismus und Idealismus* (Frankfurt, 1972), Werner Beierwaltes attempted to demonstrate that—in contrast to the general tendency of Schelling scholarship that tries to derive Schelling's thought only from theosophic influences—"there are structures of thought in Schelling and Plotinus that touch on and illustrate each other." His purpose is to "recognize the invariability of the problems posed through the similarity of the two structures of thought." The parallels that Beierwaltes points out are particularly convincing since he did not fail to show the differences between Plotinus's and Schelling's thought. Beierwaltes did not make use of the *Inquiries* in his research, but for us the problem of that which is demonic in God indicates an affinity to the theosophists. This affinity, however, would not exclude an affinity with Plotinus, because, as we have pointed out, the theosophists were in turn influenced by Neo-Platonism. Beierwaltes expressed doubts concerning the way in which Holz proceeded from "ascertainable affinity to historical 'influence'" and the way he claimed that "in place of the 'Boehme-legend'" Neo-Platonism should be substituted (p. 109).

10. Regarding this whole problem, cf. Horst Fuhrman's, *Schellings Philosophie der Weltalter* (Düsseldorf, 1954), pp. 75ff., p. 190; Jürgen Habermas, *Das Absolute und die Geschichte* (Inaugural Dissertation, 1954). Concerning the influence of Böhme, especially his doctrine of magic, cf. pp. 2ff., 7, 137, 200, 208, 210, 275ff., 256ff. Concerning Oetinger's influence pp. 128ff., 200, 208, 275ff.; Ernst Benz, *Schellings theologische Geistesahnen* (Wiesbaden, 1955); Wilhem August Schulze, "Jakob Böhme und die Kabbala," *Zeitschrift für philosophische Forschung* 9 (1955), pp. 447ff.; Karl Leese, *Vom Jakob Böhme zu Schelling: Zur Metaphysik des Gottesproblems* (Erfurt, 1922); Hans Jörg Sandkühler, *Freiheit und Wirklichkeit* (Stuttgart, 1970); Xavier Tilliette, *Schelling: Une Philosophie en Devenir* (Paris, 1970) 1:504ff.

11. As explained in this passage, there is only one way to rescue human freedom: Human freedom must be subsumed in the divine will itself, so that man's activity "also belongs to God's life" (ibid.). The very problem of the *Inquiries* is how this can be grasped in conceptual thought. It will turn out that human freedom can be determined neither outside of nor against God, nor can human freedom simply disappear in divine omnipotence (cf. 338–39). The question is thus concerned with the possibility of a "creative" (345) view of the law of identity; in other words, identity must be so determined that, as a "living" principle or as the principle of the living, it makes its opposite possible without abolishing itself as identity (ibid.).

12. In a lecture course that Martin Heidegger held in 1936 and published under the title *Schellings Abhandlung über das Wesen der menschlichen Freiheit-1809* (Tübingen, 1971), he proceeded from his own question concerning the character that Being was given at the end of traditional philosophy, in German Idealism. For him, the *Inquiries* is the pinnacle of the epoch of "subjectivity" as conceived within the history of Being (cf. p. 232).

Concerning the problem of Heideggerian "retrieving" interpretations cf. W. Marx, *Heidegger and the Tradition* (Evanston, 1960), pp. 114–17. The question, whether the theme in the *Inquiries* is the absolute freedom of God or human freedom is answered at one point so that freedom is to be viewed "not as an accessory or a feature of the human will, but rather as the essence of authentic Being [*eigentliches Seins*], as the essence of the ground for beings as a whole."

Furthermore, freedom is not taken as a property of human beings, "but rather man is at most the property of freedom." Heidegger then, however, explicitly termed freedom to be "human," for example on p. 110: "The question concerning the essence of *human* freedom leads the new 'system of freedom,'—at this point, Idealism—to waver" (cf. also p. 116). And similarly: "Freedom is, however, human freedom, and the question of a system is the question how human freedom belongs to being as a whole, i.e. to its 'ground'" (pp. 213f.). A similar statement can also be found on p. 215. And yet on p. 234 it once more becomes clear that, for Heidegger, Schelling's system of freedom is a character of Being within the history of Being, since it is only "another name for the system of subjectivity," with the one reservation that the "anthropological, consciousness-oriented interpretation of the subject" is involved (ibid.). Strangely enough, Heidegger understood the "will of love," the "allowing the ground to become effective," as a willing, a mark of "unbounded subjectivity" (p. 224), although he himself determined it to be a "calm inwardness" [*gelassene Innigheit*] (p. 225), and characterized this as a "willing of nothing, not its own and not yours, nor even itself" (ibid.).

13. Cf. on this point, J. Habermas, *Das Absolute und die Geschichte*. Habermas oriented himself toward the "historical existence of man" (p. 7). Schelling is said to pursue an "anthropological method" (pp. 225ff.), and to proceed from the microcosmos-macrocosmos analogy (pp. 227ff., p. 369). Especially relevant here are the sections "Analytic of the Human Spirit" (pp. 275ff.) and "From Absolute Identity to Historical Life" (pp. 223ff.).

14. Important first steps in this direction can, of course, already be found in the treatise *Philosophy and Religion*.

15. Cf. *Stuttgart Private Lectures* 7:423, where Schelling called the absolute or God the "principle of *all* philosophy," in contrast to the Leibniz-Wolffian and the Kantian systems, in which God is "brought in only at the end." The absolute is not only a principle in the sense of that which is highest or primary, as the supreme "ground of explanation for all things," and by no means can it be seen as a "particular object" as it is in theology. God or the absolute is more than that, it is the "element in which alone demonstration is possible" (ibid.). "Everything can only be presented *within* the absolute" (ibid.). Philosophy thus does not have the absolute as its object, the absolute's existence is not something that philosophy would have to first of all prove, in order to be able to begin; philosophy is rather *itself* the "continuing proof of the absolute." "Proof" means manifestation here, but only in that sense in which philosophy is incorporated in the occurrence of the absolute's *self-manifestation*. As "mental presentation" [*geistige Darstellung*] of the absolute in its revelation in the universe, philosophy is a part of "God's continual proving of himself." Schelling, therefore, did not simply say that philosophy is a philosophy of the absolute because it conceives of the absolute and makes the absolute its principle of explanation for all things. Instead he conceived of the relationship to the absolute so that philosophy belongs to the absolute and not the absolute to philosophy.

16. Cf. W. Marx, *Hegel's Phenomenology of Spirit* (New York, 1975).

17. After this essay had been completed, Guido Vergauwen's *Absolute und endliche Freiheit* (Freiburg, Switzerland, 1975) appeared, which deals with Schelling's entire work on the basis of the problem of freedom. It also contains an extensive section on the *Inquiries*. I am for the most part in agreement with

Vergauwen's interpretation, although the subject of the *Inquiries* for him is not an "ontology of life," as we would suggest, but rather an ontology of love (pp. 130, 156, 186). Since, in my opinion too, life as absolute freedom is of course realized as love in accordance with the ultimate intention of creation, this difference of opinion is not of great significance. What I wish to stress is the way in which the ultimate intention of creation concretely realizes itself with the assistance of finite freedom which espouses evil.

18. The expression "leap" [*Sprung*] is employed by Schelling in *Philosophy and Religion* (VI, 38) in the discussion of the question of whether and how a transition from the absolute (infinitude) into finitude can be made. Here Schelling critically addressed himself to the doctrine of emanation, in which finitude came to be through a continual effluence from infinity. The expression as used in *Philosophy and Religion* does not refer to the question of divine self-constitution in freedom. There is, however, an essential relatedness here insofar as this "leap" is a characterization of the *freedom* of God's "likeness" [*Gegenbild*], of "the other absolute," to "its freedom to 'grasp itself in its selfhood'" (ibid.) and thus to "fall" from the absolute (cf. 40).

19. In *The Ages of the World* (1813–14), we see how this determination of the absolute as life extends beyond itself and leads to a new determination of freedom within the dimension of the absolute. If "life" is understood as the "movement" of the absolute's becoming a "being," if life is taken in its strict ontological meaning, then "beyond" this life, the self-revelation of the absolute as freedom must be conceived of as freedom in an eminent sense: as that freedom which is truly absolute, the freedom to be or not to be. This is "the pure (*lautere*) freedom itself" (VIII, 237), the pure will that wills nothing and is to this extent also not a willing (ibid.); it is freedom as the state of "indifference" toward all Being and non-Being, which nevertheless is not simply nothing, but rather that which retains position and negation within itself; and by being capable of doing so, is *command over itself*. Schelling conceived of freedom here not only as the absolute freedom of the deed of self-revelation, but also as the "state" of the absolute in which the principles of self-revelation (the principles of Being) are preserved.

20. Cf. Gershom Sholem, *Über einige Grundbegriffe des Judentums* (Frankfurt, 1970), pp. 53ff.; Gershom Sholem, *Die jüdische Mystik und ihre Hauptströmungen* (Frankfurt, 1967) pp. 285–90.

21. Cf. VII, 384, where Schelling rejected the Kantian concept of self-determination (at least on his interpretation), because in it the transition from "pure and simple indeterminacy" to determinacy remains unexplained and leads to a concept of freedom as mere "willful choice."

22. Cf. also *Stuttgart Private Lectures* VII:429ff., and *Philosophy and Religion* VII:41f., where the "fall" is characterized as an active deed.

23. Cf. I. Kant, *Religion within the Bounds of Reason*, in Kant, *Werke*, Akademie Textausgabe, (Berlin, 1968) VI, p. 37.

24. According to Habermas, *Das Absolute und die Geschichte*, Schelling's investigations into human freedom led to the "breakthrough of a specific understanding of historicity." Schelling is said to have "expanded the horizon of the historicity of the finite spirit . . ." (Cf. p. 5, 7, 9, 11). Concerning the question of history and historicity as a whole, cf. pp. 203, 266ff., 313, 319ff. Besides this dissertation, which was essentially determined by Heideggerian problems, cf.

the essay "Dialektischer Idealismus im Übergang zum Materialismus— Geschichtsphilosophische Folgerungen aus Schellings Idee einer Kontraktion Gottes," *Theorie und Praxis* (Frankfurt, 1971) pp. 172ff., where the *Inquiries* imply the "abandonment of the absolute to history" (p. 194); the corrupted world is "a world which has fallen from God's control" (p. 193), a world whose history has been entrusted to the "God in reverse," mankind as a social being. "For the sake of love," God had to accept the danger that his image might fail him, and that the bond of forces in fact would be dissolved, which in God is indissoluable (ibid.). Habermas failed to see the eschatological construction of the *Inquiries* and the fact that, for Schelling, creation has an "ultimate intention" (cf. VII, 403–404 and 404–405), the fact that, in the end, God will be all in all (405–406), since there must be a final separation of evil from good in the "perfect actualization of God." If God will then through love have taken power over the condition of his existence, the ground, and subordinated it to his glorification, one cannot speak of an abandonment of the absolute to history. Only if one neglects the explicitly eschatological character of the *Inquiries* can one come to the particular "conclusion of a philosophy of history on the basis of the idea of a divine contraction" (pp. 194ff), which Habermas used to develop certain affiliations to Marx, and which he uses to determine the social task of man. Cf. on this point above p. 61, note 7.

25. W. Beierwaltes, *Platonismus und Idealismus*, defended another view of the determination "all in all" as the dialectical dimension of everything particular.

26. Cf. *Stuttgart Private Lectures*, VII, 428.

INDEX OF PROPER NAMES

INDEX OF SUBJECTS